Learning LEGO MINDSTORMS EV3

Build and create interactive, sensor-based robots using your LEGO MINDSTORMS EV3 kit

Gary Garber

BIRMINGHAM - MUMBAI

Learning LEGO MINDSTORMS EV3

Copyright © 2015 Packt Publishing

First published: January 2015

Production reference: 1200115

Published by Packt Publishing Ltd.
Livery Place
35 Livery Street
Birmingham B3 2PB, UK.

ISBN 978-1-78398-502-9

www.packtpub.com

Cover image by Gary Garber

Credits

About the Author

Gary Garber teaches physics, math, and engineering at Boston University Academy. Gary is the president of the New England Section of the American Association of Physics Teachers and has led dozens of professional development workshops in education at both the local and national levels.

Gary runs the Boston University FIRST Robotics program. He has run and hosted numerous robotics workshops in VEX, Tetrix, and LEGO platforms. He has run dozens of LEGO robotics tournaments and spoken on robotics education at both local and national conferences. His robotics team has worked with Engineers Without Borders, NASA, and the National Science Teachers Association on a variety of engineering and education projects.

He is currently an educational consultant, working to develop new software tools for the classroom, at the Tufts Center for Engineering Education and Outreach, which is a pioneer in LEGO Robotics Education. He is the author of *Instant LEGO MINDSTORMS EV3*, *Packt Publishing*. He currently resides in Massachusetts, US. When he is not playing with LEGO, robots, or toy trains, he enjoys spending time with his wife, Catalina, and their two children, Alejandro and Leonardo.

I would like to thank the people of the Tufts Center for Engineering Education and Outreach for teaching me about LEGO robotics and helping make this book possible, including Chris Rogers, Ethan Danahy, Barbara Bratzel, and Bill Church. I would like to thank the students of Boston University Academy, in particular, the class of 2016, who remind me of how much fun students of all ages can have with LEGO. I would also like to thank Alejandro and Leonardo for reteaching me how to play with LEGO and making me watch the LEGO movie over and over again.

About the Reviewers

Barbara Bratzel is a science teacher at the Shady Hill School, a PreK-8 independent school in Cambridge, Massachusetts. In addition, she is a consulting teacher at the Center for Engineering Education and Outreach at Tufts University. Her most recent book, *STEM by Design*, a collection of classroom activities using the LEGO EV3, was published in February 2014.

Michael duPont is a maker, pilot, and theatre technician based in Central Florida. He recently graduated from Centre College in Danville, Kentucky. His specialties include microcontrollers such as the Raspberry Pi and Arduino, robotics, wearables, and other small electronics. You can find many of his open source projects on GitHub and on his website (http://mdupont.com/).

Jeroen Hartsuiker (born in 1971) played with LEGO Technic until his early teens. His dark ages (time when a person stops collecting and using the Danish bricks) ended while visiting LEGOLAND Billund in 1998, when he attended a workshop exploring the first generation of the MINDSTORMS Robotics Invention System. Since then, he has owned and used every generation of the LEGO robot, and he wrote courseware and delivered a presentation on how to control the MINDSTORMS NXT robot using Microsoft® Robotics Developer Studio. He occasionally contributes a module to the **Great Ball Contraption (GBC)** at LEGO WORLD in the Netherlands. Furthermore, a MINDSTORMS robot is sometimes used to make the software-development classes he teaches even more interesting. You can visit his blog at www.dotnetjes.nl.

David Lechner works mostly as a freelance computer programmer and occasionally as a "Mad Scientist" teaching robotics as an after-school program in elementary schools. He also just completed his rookie year, coaching a FIRST LEGO League team, and has devoted much of his time to reverse engineering the EV3 as a core contributor to the ev3dev project. Prior to being self-employed, he spent 8 years doing industrial automation in the water and wastewater industry. He has a bachelor's degree in electrical and computer engineering from Oklahoma State University.

Diego "Kartones" Muñoz, more commonly known by his nickname, Kartones, is a multidisciplinary developer who lives in Madrid, Spain. Having worked for more than 12 years with all kinds of desktop, mobile, and web applications, he has used quite a few languages such as C++, C#, PHP, and more recently, Ruby and JavaScript.

Regarding LEGO MINDSTORMS, he fell in love with RCX and then the NXT, both of which he liked to code in C instead of the default firmware and brick system. Now, with MINDSTORMS EV3, he seeks to code robot logic in Node.js. He's also been a technical reviewer for *LEGO Mindstorms EV3 Essentials, Packt Publishing*.

He loves learning about anything he comes across and keeps a few blogs. He sometimes speaks at events or user groups, and he would love to do more open source work. He can be reached at `http://portfolio.kartones.net`.

I'd like to acknowledge my girlfriend and my cats, for without their patience with my endless hours around computers and technology, I wouldn't be so happy.

Geoff Shannon has been an enthusiastic hardware hacker from a young age; his first job was building automated production equipment with Provel Inc. He has a bachelor's degree in computer science and recently attended a batch at Hacker School in New York City. In late 2013, he started working with LEGO robots by exploring the leJOS project and using it to run a Clojure REPL on his EV3. He currently lives in Seattle, WA, working as a software engineer.

To see what Geoff is currently working on and thinking about, check out his blog at www.zephyrizing.net. You can also follow him on Twitter at @RadicalZephyr.

www.PacktPub.com

Support files, eBooks, discount offers, and more

For support files and downloads related to your book, please visit www.PacktPub.com.

Did you know that Packt offers eBook versions of every book published, with PDF and ePub files available? You can upgrade to the eBook version at www.PacktPub.com and as a print book customer, you are entitled to a discount on the eBook copy. Get in touch with us at service@packtpub.com for more details.

At www.PacktPub.com, you can also read a collection of free technical articles, sign up for a range of free newsletters and receive exclusive discounts and offers on Packt books and eBooks.

https://www2.packtpub.com/books/subscription/packtlib

Do you need instant solutions to your IT questions? PacktLib is Packt's online digital book library. Here, you can search, access, and read Packt's entire library of books.

Why subscribe?

- Fully searchable across every book published by Packt
- Copy and paste, print, and bookmark content
- On demand and accessible via a web browser

Free access for Packt account holders

If you have an account with Packt at www.PacktPub.com, you can use this to access PacktLib today and view 9 entirely free books. Simply use your login credentials for immediate access.

Table of Contents

Preface

Welcome to *Learning LEGO MINDSTORMS EV3*.

The LEGO MINDSTORMS EV3 is a programmable LEGO brick that can control motors and receive feedback from a wide range of sensors. In this book, you will learn how to write programs in the LEGO MINDSTORMS EV3 software. This book is a practical guide that will show you how to advance beyond the basic lessons included in your EV3 kit, combine core programming commands, and implement tested design principles when building your own robot using the LEGO MINDSTORMS EV3 kit. You will become familiar with resources beyond your EV3 kit and enhance your robot designs.

The MINDSTORMS EV3 kit contains over 500 plastic interlocking parts. These parts are made with high-precision moulds. The LEGO Technic bricks in your kit include beams, axles, pines, gears, shafts, and bushings that will allow you to design a wide variety of robots. The LEGO bricks in your LEGO MINDSTORMS kit are compatible with all LEGO bricks made over the past 50 years.

The LEGO MINDSTORMS EV3 Intelligent Brick contains an ARM9 processor running Linux. This allows you to program the brick with a wide variety of languages, such as C, C++, Java, Python, and LabVIEW, but we will focus on the official LEGO MINDSTORMS EV3 software. This software is a visual programming language. Programming in the LEGO MINDSTORMS EV3 software consists of dragging-and-dropping blocks onto a programming canvas. You draw wires to connect the command blocks, such as command flow wires and data wires. There are blocks that store data, control motors, acquire sensor data, and initiate flow structures such as loops and switches. The beauty of a visual programming language is that with a programming hierarchy, you can create easy-to-follow programs where you can visually see the entire program at once.

The EV3 Intelligent Brick connects to motors and a wide variety of sensors, which LEGO builds via electrical wires, including Touch Sensors, Ultrasonic Sensors, Light Sensors, Infrared Sensors, and Gyro Sensors. The motors have built-in shaft encoders, which allow you to control exactly how far they turn. There is an even larger array of sensors produced by third-party vendors that you can use with your EV3. You can download and run your computer programs on the EV3 via a USB cable, Bluetooth, or Wi-Fi. All these features will take your LEGO MINDSTORMS EV3 beyond the category of a simple toy into an impressive robotics kit, which can be used to explore your environment and navigate a complex set of obstacles.

What this book covers

Chapter 1, Engineering Notebook, covers how to use the Content Editor to keep a multimedia record of your work building robots.

Chapter 2, Mechanical Design, covers how to use gears to increase either speed or torque in your robots.

Chapter 3, Drive Train and Chassis, explains how to build a chassis and attach either wheels or treads to create a moving robot.

Chapter 4, Sensors and Control, covers how to use sensors to receive feedback from your environment.

Chapter 5, Interacting with EV3, explains how to control your EV3 via the brick buttons, the infrared beacon, Bluetooth, and Wi-Fi.

Chapter 6, Output from EV3, covers how to send output from the EV3 brick using the display screen, lights, and the speaker.

Chapter 7, Advanced Programming, covers topics such as loops, switches, arrays, My Blocks, and navigation using sensor feedback.

Chapter 8, Advanced Programming and Control, covers advanced navigation techniques, including proportional controllers, PID controllers, course correction, and triangulation.

Chapter 9, Experiment Software and Data Logging, explains how to use the data logging features of the Educational Edition of the LEGO MINDSTORMS software.

Chapter 10, Other Programming Languages, provides a brief overview of RobotC and LabVIEW, which are the next steps up from using the LEGO MINDSTORMS software.

Chapter 11, Communication between Robots, explains how to send messages via Bluetooth to allow two EV3 robots to communicate, send commands, and collaborate.

Chapter 12, Advanced Robot – Gyro Boy, reviews and explains in depth the Gyro Boy program written by LEGO.

What you need for this book

You will need a LEGO MINDSTORMS EV3 kit to build the robots in this book. There are two versions of the kit: the LEGO MINDSTORMS EV3 Home Edition (Lego Set # 31313) and the LEGO MINDSTORMS EV3 Education Core Set (Lego Set # 45544). Both of these kits can be purchased for about $350. I have provided build instructions in this book, so you can build your robots no matter which set you have. The hardware differences include the type of wheels, treads, and casters. Between the kits, most of the pieces are the same but of different colors. The Home Edition has a Touch Sensor, Color Sensor, Infrared Sensor, and Infrared beacon. The Education Edition has a Touch Sensor, Color Sensor, Gyro Sensor, Ultrasonic Sensor, and a rechargeable battery. You can buy all of these parts at http://shop.lego.com/en-US/ or any general toy supplier.

If they did not come with your kit, you may want to buy the following:

- EV3 rechargeable battery (Part # 45501), which is $60
- EV3 Ultrasonic Sensor (Part # 45504), which is $30
- EV3 Infrared Sensor (Part # 45509), which is $30
- EV3 Infrared beacon (Part # 45508), which is $30
- EV3 Gyro Sensor (Part # 45505), which is $30

You will need the LEGO MINDSTORMS EV3 software. There are two versions of the software. The Home Edition of the software is free and can be downloaded from www.lego.com/mindstorms. The Education Edition of the software needs to be purchased from LEGO Education for $100 from https://education.lego.com. The main differences between the software editions are that the Education Edition includes data logging software and the aesthetics of the splash page. This book was written with version 1.1.1 of the LEGO MINDSTORMS EV3 software. At the time of publication, version 1.1.1 is only available for the Home Edition. The Education Edition is currently available in version 1.1.0. As a caution, in version 1.1.0 of the LEGO MINDSTORMS software, Bluetooth communication for the EV3 brick is not compatible with newer versions of Mac OS X.

You will receive the most bang-for-your-buck by purchasing the Education Edition of the hardware kit from LEGO Education and downloading the Home Edition of the software. Besides http://www.amazon.com/, you will find the best secondary market to purchase LEGO bricks at http://bricklink.com/.

Who this book is for

The LEGO MINDSTORMS software has built-in tutorials that explain very basic usage of the software. The tutorials also provide high-end examples of what can potentially be built with the MINDSTORMS kits. The programs written to accompany these high-end examples are wonderfully complex, but lacking in documentation. A major gap in the materials provided by LEGO is that they do not help you past those first simple steps to build and program advanced robots.

This book is for anyone who wants to develop his or her LEGO MINDSTORMS EV3 robots past those first simple steps. I assume you have gone through the basic tutorials provided by LEGO. I provide build instructions for a base robot to which you can add sensors and work through the advanced programming algorithms provided in this book. Students and coaches working with FIRST LEGO League teams and World Robot Olympiad teams will benefit from using the techniques described in this book to develop their ability to navigate a playing field using sensors.

Conventions

In this book, you will find a number of styles of text that distinguish between different kinds of information.

New terms and **important words** are shown in bold. Words that you see on the screen, in menus or dialog boxes for example, appear in the text like this: "Do not press the **Finish** button yet."

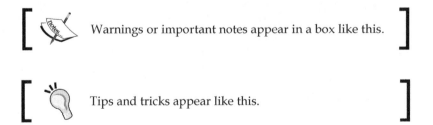

Warnings or important notes appear in a box like this.

Tips and tricks appear like this.

Reader feedback

Feedback from our readers is always welcome. Let us know what you think about this book—what you liked or disliked. Reader feedback is important for us as it helps us develop titles that you will really get the most out of.

To send us general feedback, simply e-mail feedback@packtpub.com, and mention the book's title in the subject of your message.

If there is a topic that you have expertise in and you are interested in either writing or contributing to a book, see our author guide at www.packtpub.com/authors.

Customer support

Now that you are the proud owner of a Packt book, we have a number of things to help you to get the most from your purchase.

Downloading the example code

You can download the example code files from your account at http://www.packtpub.com for all the Packt Publishing books you have purchased. If you purchased this book elsewhere, you can visit http://www.packtpub.com/support and register to have the files e-mailed directly to you.

Downloading the color images of this book

We also provide you with a PDF file that has color images of the screenshots/diagrams used in this book. The color images will help you better understand the changes in the output. You can download this file from: https://www.packtpub.com/sites/default/files/downloads/5029OS_ColoredImages.pdf.

Errata

Although we have taken every care to ensure the accuracy of our content, mistakes do happen. If you find a mistake in one of our books—maybe a mistake in the text or the code—we would be grateful if you could report this to us. By doing so, you can save other readers from frustration and help us improve subsequent versions of this book. If you find any errata, please report them by visiting http://www.packtpub.com/submit-errata, selecting your book, clicking on the **Errata Submission Form** link, and entering the details of your errata. Once your errata are verified, your submission will be accepted and the errata will be uploaded to our website or added to any list of existing errata under the Errata section of that title.

To view the previously submitted errata, go to https://www.packtpub.com/books/
content/support and enter the name of the book in the search field. The required
information will appear under the **Errata** section.

Piracy

Piracy of copyrighted material on the Internet is an ongoing problem across all
media. At Packt, we take the protection of our copyright and licenses very seriously.
If you come across any illegal copies of our works in any form on the Internet, please
provide us with the location address or website name immediately so that we can
pursue a remedy.

Please contact us at copyright@packtpub.com with a link to the suspected
pirated material.

We appreciate your help in protecting our authors and our ability to bring
you valuable content.

Questions

If you have a problem with any aspect of this book, you can contact us at
questions@packtpub.com, and we will do our best to address the problem.

1
Engineering Notebook

As described by LEGO, the EV3 MINDSTORMS software **Content Editor** is a digital workbook into which you can enter text, images, sound, and videos. There are a lot of great features that are described in brief by LEGO in the EV3 software help menus. In this chapter, we will look at the following topics:

- The engineering design process
- Advanced features of the Content Editor
- How to add images into the Content Editor
- How to add pages and page actions
- Computer Aided Design and adding building instructions
- How to add comments into your programs

The engineering design process

Without using those words, with the Content Editor, LEGO has created a digital engineering notebook. An engineering notebook is more than just a record of your work. An engineering notebook allows you to record (and communicate) your initial designs, construct the model, and iterate your building and programming. In the engineering design process, it is important to record your mistakes so that you have a record of what didn't work. You should always put dates on the work you have done.

According to the U.S. Next Generation Science Standards, we can present a simplified version of the engineering process in the following diagram:

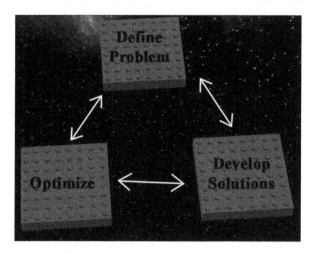

The process of iteration and optimization is critical to building good models. Particularly when it comes to programming, you will find you need to make numerous revisions to your program so that your robot has the desired performance. The preceding image is an abbreviated version of what is often presented as the engineering design process. There is no single engineering design process. There are many variations on the preceding theme, starting with a problem and ending with a solution. The common steps include the following:

1. Defining the problem.
2. Researching the problem and the constraints.
3. Brainstorming to develop several possible solutions.
4. Selecting one solution.
5. Drawing and building prototypes.
6. Testing and evaluating.
7. Redesigning and optimizing.

The iterative nature of the engineering design process is important. Often, if will not follow a straightforward path between these steps. With this number of steps, you need to document your work and record successes and distresses. Additionally, the evolution of thought and the solutions for one challenge might easily be translated to another. The Content Editor built into the EV3 software easily fulfills the task of a multimedia-based engineering notebook.

Content Editor features

When you start a new project in the EV3 software, the Content Editor will automatically open up on the upper right-hand side of the Programming Canvas.

The Content Editor will automatically open up in View mode, as shown in the preceding screenshot. If you click on the Pencil icon (encircled in the preceding screenshot), you can switch from View mode to Edit mode; this allows you to enter information.

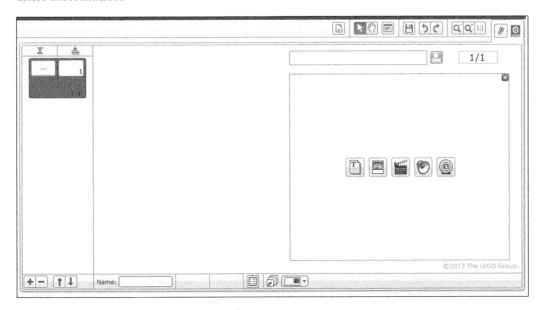

When entering Edit mode, the EV3 software limits the icons displayed to five basic functions such as Text and Image. You can access the full range of the Content Editor functions by clicking on the red cross sign in the upper right-hand corner:

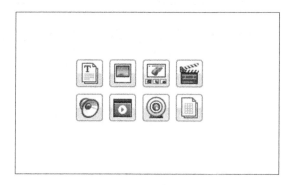

The basic features of the Content Editor, shown in the preceding screenshot, include (going clockwise from the top) Text, Image, Building Instructions, Video, Table, Webcam, Document, and Sound. If you want to return to the abbreviated version of this menu, you can click on the Document icon. By themselves, many of these entries might seem limited. However, using the selections in Page Setup, you can combine these features into a powerful record of your work.

When you create a new page in the Content Editor (by clicking on the plus sign), it will open up the templates shown in the following screenshot:

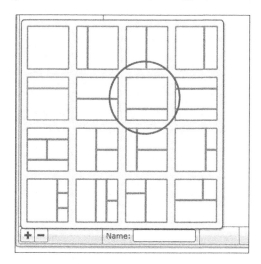

I particularly like to have text on the bottom panel to describe to the reader what they are looking at in any videos and images, or building instructions on the top panel. If you click on the icon I have circled in red in the previous screenshot, you will see two panels appear as shown in the following screenshot:

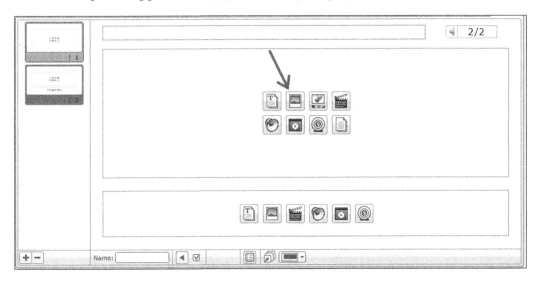

Next, let's insert an image into the top window in the Content Editor. Click on the Image icon. When working with the image, you will find that you can only upload JPG and PNG images. Then try typing some text into the bottom window after clicking on the Text icon, as shown in the following screenshot:

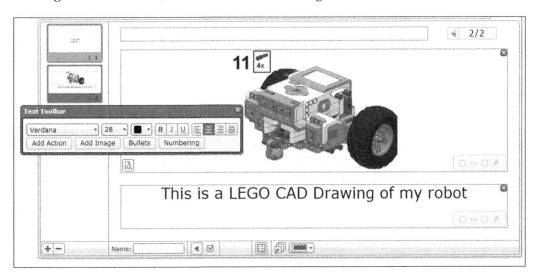

You will see that the **Text Toolbar** allows you to set the fonts and the formatting. When working with text, I like to add text actions. If you click on **Add Action**, encircled in the following screenshot, several options are presented:

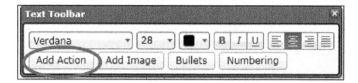

A drop-down menu will appear with these options as shown in the following screenshot. The actions are similar to a hyperlink. They allow you to open programs or a website with the page or move to a different page. This is particularly useful if you have numerous pages in the Content Editor for your program. For example, you could create a table of contents at the beginning.

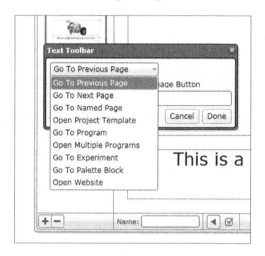

After you have created several pages, you should try to use the function **Go To Named Page**. A good use for naming your pages is to create dates so that you know when you did your work. You might choose to name your pages with the date you created it on. I also like the **Go To Program** option. At this point, the EV3 software Version 1.1 doesn't allow you to choose programs that are part of a different project. You can also use a **Text Button** to emphasize the text action, as shown in the following screenshot:

New pages and page actions

Embedded into the EV3 software are model instructions for several different robots. These instructions are presented in the Content Editor and follow a certain format spread out over three pages.

- A video of the completed model
- Step-by-step building instructions
- The computer program

However, the program does not appear until you reach the third page. The mechanism to allow this is called **Page Action**. By moving to the next page, you can trigger actions such as opening a program or project. This is useful if you don't want your reader to be distracted by what is coming next, or you want it to be a surprise. In order to trigger the release of a program, follow the steps shown in the following screenshots. First open the **Page Action** menu.

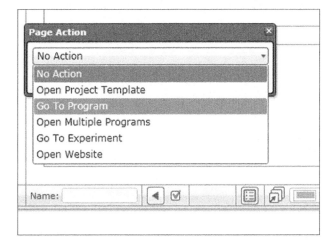

If you select **Go To Program**, then you will be asked to choose a program, as shown in the following screenshot, so that, when the page is opened, the program will open simultaneously. This can also be useful if you are using different programs for the same model. For instance, you could include a video and/or text description of the execution of that program in a page of the Content Editor, but not open the program until the page is selected.

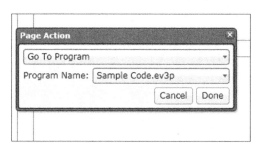

Computer-aided Design and building instructions

Using **Computer-aided Design (CAD)** software can be useful on several fronts. Once you learn how to use this kind of software, you will find it can be quicker to build models digitally than with real bricks. Real engineers always design their robots virtually before building the actual product. This is because the process of trial and error involved with trying to fit parts together can be time consuming and expensive. If you have a large inventory of (unorganized) LEGO bricks beyond those included in your EV3 kit, you might build something digitally before you go searching for the bricks. At this point, it is worth mentioning the two most common CAD programs: LEGO Digital Designer and LDraw.

LEGO Digital Designer

LEGO produces **LEGO Digital Design (LDD)** and it is a free download. LDD was designed for children, you can use it to build instructions. LDD exports its build instructions as HTML files or .png files. An image of LDD is shown in the following screenshot. Bricks snap together with LDD, but precision is necessary. Additionally, you may have trouble aligning gears with LDD. You will need to rotate them to make them fit. If the pieces do not align in the software, it will not let you put the piece into place. You can download LDD from http://ldd.lego.com/.

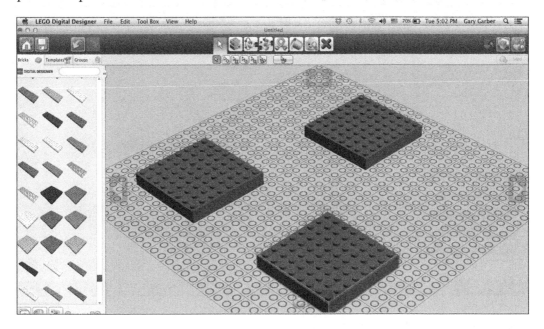

LDraw

LDraw (LEGO Draw) is a file format specification used by a large number of advanced LEGO CAD programs. The LDraw standard is free and open source. In the following screenshot, you can see the software I used to write this book, **MLCad**. You can precisely define the exact location and rotation of every LEGO brick. Bricks do not automatically snap together as in LDD, but with gears you might need this flexibility. LDraw-based CAD programs also have a larger parts library compared to LDD.

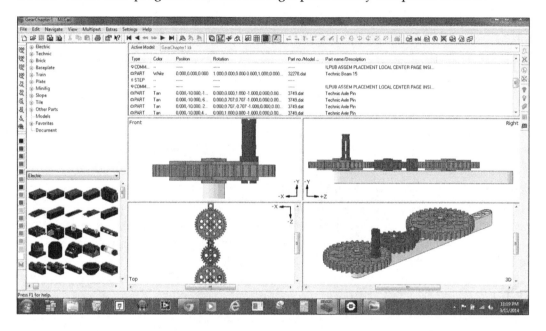

You can also define the viewpoint of your model when creating building instructions. The capabilities of LDraw programs are far more advanced (than LDD). **LEGO Publisher (LPub)** is another piece of free and open source software that generates building instructions with step numbers. **Mike's LEGO Computer-aided Design (MLCAD)** in combination with LPub produced the images shown in the following screenshot. As you can see, the Bill of Materials for the model is imported into EV3 software from LPub.

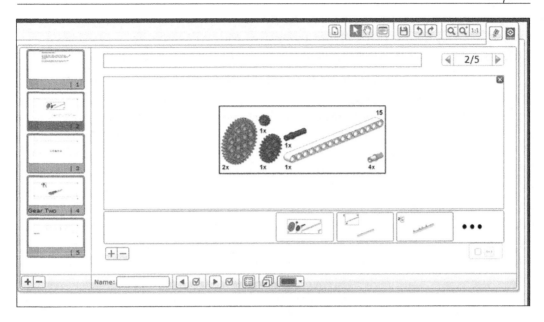

In the next screenshot, you can see one of the building steps imported into the EV3 software. At the bottom of the screenshot, you can see several of the building steps. If you click on a building step, it will highlight that step. The difference between an Image Page and a Building Instruction Page in the Content Editor is that the Building Instruction Page lets you have multiple images on one page.

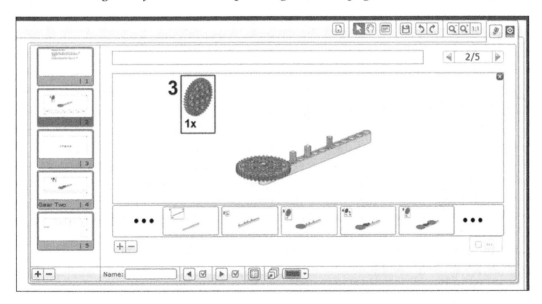

After you have inserted the build instructions into the EV3 software, you can look at them in View mode. You will find the instructions large enough to be usable. This is very useful as a record for yourself and to communicate to others what you have done!

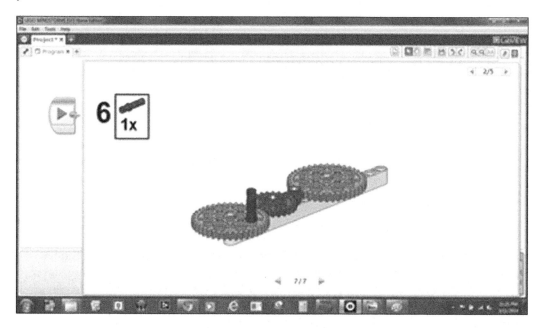

 You can download LDraw type software from www.ldraw.org.

Commenting on your code

Although not part of the Content Editor, annotating the actual programming code is incredibly important. Not only does this serve as a record of your own work, but also others who read your programs will understand what you are thinking. And, as you work through iterations of your programming, commenting allows you to mark any changes you make to the program. Traditional computer languages have comment lines to explain the code. As a visual programming language, the EV3 MINDSTORMS software allows you to add comment boxes near the relevant algorithms. If you click on the **Comment** icon I have circled in red in the following screenshot, a small comment box will appear. You will need to increase the size of the comment box in order to type words into it. You can then move the comment box around the programming window to the appropriate place in your code.

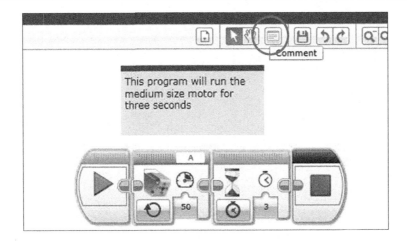

Summary

In this chapter, you have learned about some of the advanced features of the Content Editor, about the engineering process, to upload images and building instructions, and to annotate your work.

In the next chapter, we will build gear trains using several types of gears. You will learn how to increase the speed or power of your motors using a set of gears.

2
Mechanical Design

In this chapter, we will build and program several models to demonstrate the basic principles of mechanical design. We will:

- Explore the idea of mechanical advantage
- Learn how you can increase either speed or torque using different combinations of gears
- Build gearboxes with motors
- Use the spur gears, beveled gears, and worm gears
- Write a program to spin the motors a set number of rotations
- Use the display on the EV3 brick

All of the models in this chapter can be built with both the EV3 Home Edition and EV3 Educational Edition kits.

Mechanical advantage

When designing a robot, sometimes we may want to build a fast robot that needs to get to its objective quickly. At other times, we may want a powerful robot. For instance, maybe the robot needs to push a heavy object, push another robot, or climb a steep hill. When it comes to a robotic arm, we might be trying to lift a heavy object slowly or lift a small object quickly.

However, we cannot have both speed and power. There is a trade-off here—if you increase one, you decrease the other. This trade-off is called the law of conservation of energy.

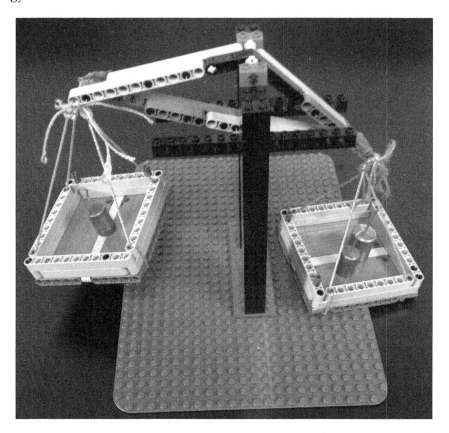

LEGO bricks allow us to use several types of simple machines. The simplest would be the lever arm. You can easily create a lever with LEGO beams and pins. To balance a seesaw or a lever, the amount of torque or rotational force must be the same on either side of the seesaw. In the preceding image, we see a LEGO balance with unequal forces but equal lever arms. The longer the lever arm, the less force we need to rotate the lever. In the following image, we have doubled the length of the lever arm on the left but the mass is only half the size.

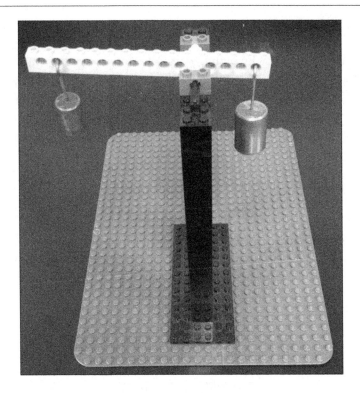

We define the mechanical advantage using Archimedes' Law of the Lever. The **mechanical advantage** is the length of the longer lever divided by the length of the shorter lever. The lever in the preceding image has a mechanical advantage of 2 because we have doubled the length.

$$MA = \frac{Length_{output}}{Length_{input}}$$

A longer lever arm will increase our mechanical advantage. If the mechanical advantage is greater than 1, the output of our machine will have an increase in force over the input.

The Home Edition of the EV3 kit comes with rubber bands, which can be used in a pulley system. In the LEGO MINDSTORMS kits, the most common way to increase your mechanical advantage is by using gears. We can assemble two or more gears together in what is called a **gear train**. The teeth of gears will mesh together. We can define the mechanical advantage in a gear train by the number of teeth, N, on each gear.

$$MA = \frac{N_{output}}{N_{input}}$$

If the number of teeth on the output gear is greater than the number of teeth on the input gear, the mechanical advantage is greater than one. This will result in more torque or rotational force on the output of our gear train. However, the rotational speed, ω, decreases in the same ratio as torque increases.

$$\frac{\omega_{input}}{\omega_{output}} = \frac{N_{output}}{N_{input}}$$

Motors

The EV3 kit comes with two large motors and one medium motor. Beyond the packaging, there are some other important differences between the large motor and the medium motor. The following list compares the features of the large and medium motor:

- Large motor maximum speed 170 rpm
- Medium motor maximum speed 250 rpm
- Large motor torque when rotating 0.21 N·m (Newton-meters is a unit used to measure torque)
- Medium motor torque when rotating 0.08 N·m
- Large motor torque at standstill 0.42 N·m
- Medium motor torque at standstill 0.12 N·m
- Large motor mass is 76 grams
- Medium motor mass is 36 grams

The large motor will be excellent to power the drive train of our robot, and if you need the extra speed, you can always gear the motors up. If you need more torque, you can gear down. The medium motor is about half the mass of the large motor. The medium motor actually spins about 50 percent faster than the large motor. The torque of the medium motor is only a fraction of the large motor. This makes the medium motor ideal for lighter loads.

Large motors and gears

We will be building a simple gear train with two gears powered by the large motor. The gears we are using are double bevel gears. Normally, when you think of a gear, you are thinking of a straight or a spur gear. The LEGO double bevel gear is essentially a spur gear in the middle, with beveled edges on both sides. Not only does this allow you to combine two double bevel gears aligned parallel to each other as we are in this section, but you can also combine them at right angles, as we will see later in this chapter. I chose this particular set of gears because they are included in both the Home Edition and Educational Edition kits. However, you could build a gear train like this using any set of dissimilar gears. The small gear has 12 teeth, and the large gear has 36 teeth. The motor will power the larger gear. We will find that every time the large gear spins once, the small gear will spin three times. So we are gaining speed, but at the cost of losing torque. This gives us a mechanical advantage of one third. So at full power, our small gear could rotate at a speed of about 500 rpm.

You will need the following parts to build this model. The only piece that is different between the two EV3 kits is the 11-mod beam; it's white in the Educational Edition and red (shown in the following screenshot) in the Home Edition.

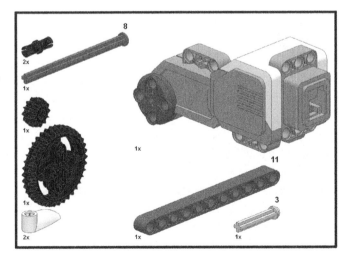

In the following four steps, we will build a simple gear train:

1. First, insert an 8-mod stopped axle through the larger motor and two friction pins.

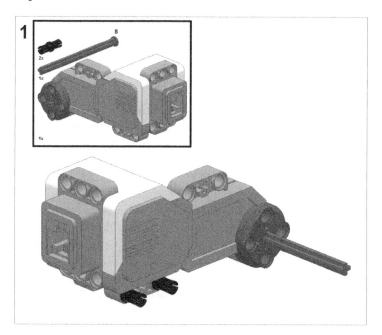

2. Next attach a 3-mod stopped axle and the 11-mod beam.

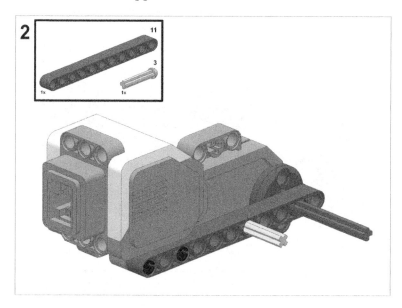

3. Now, we will attach the large and small double-bevel gears to the axles.

4. In the next step we will add two flag bricks.

The flag will allow us to visualize easily how many times each motor has rotated. When you run the program, you will see that the gear with the small flag will rotate three times as fast as the large gear. You can of course also add more gears to the beam. You should note that the gears in this model turn in opposite directions. Every time you add a gear, it will turn in the opposite direction of the gear it is next to. So if you were to add a third gear, it will turn in the same direction as the original gear.

Writing a program

After we attach the cables, we will be ready to write a program to make the motor spin. Connect the motor to port D on your EV3 brick. Turn on your EV3 brick by pressing the dark gray button in the center of the brick.

After you start up the EV3 software, navigate to **File | New Project | Program**. This will start up a new program. You could easily start one of the many LEGO tutorials at this point. We will start with a blank sheet. The startup menu you see in the following screenshot is the main difference between the Home Edition version of the software and the Educational Edition. Additionally, the Home Edition does not allow you to do experiments.

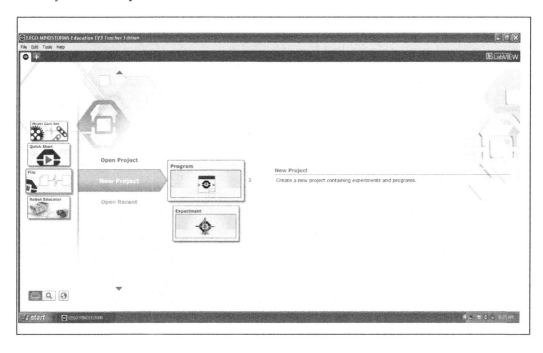

You will see several icons at the bottom of the screen on the green Action tab of the Programming Palette. Drag a Large Motor block (encircled in red in the following screenshot) onto the Programming Canvas and place it next to the Start block.

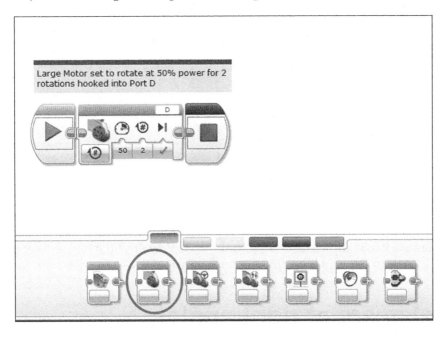

Although not required, you can add a Stop block at the end of the program. You can find the Stop block on the dark blue Advanced tab of the Programming Palette, as added in the following screenshot:

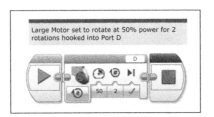

We will now set up the Large Motor block:

- Using the drop-down menu, set the Large Motor block to **On for Rotations**
- Set the number of rotations of the wheels to 2
- The power level is set to **50** percent
- The motor is set to port **D**

The motors have built-in shaft encoders that can tell how far the motors have rotated.

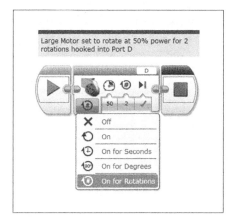

Your EV3 brick should be powered on. Make sure your robot is connected to your computer via the USB cable. Next, click on the Download and Run button. Your large gear will make two complete rotations, and the small gear will make six complete rotations. You can also run it by clicking on the Start block.

Bevel gears at right angles

In the next example, we are going to build a gearbox using a 12-tooth bevel gear along with the large 36 tooth straight gear with double bevels. These gears actually rotate at right angles to each other. Since the motor drives the smaller gear, the output of our gearbox is actually slower than the motor. However, we will gain torque in this system, so we have a mechanical advantage of 3. We will be using the medium motor in this model.

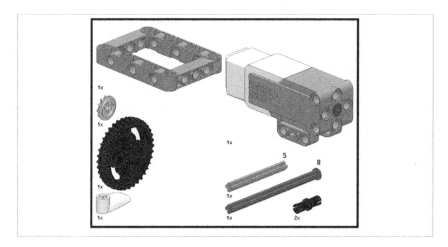

In the following five steps, we will build a gearbox with two gears at right angles:

1. First attach two friction pins to the medium motor.

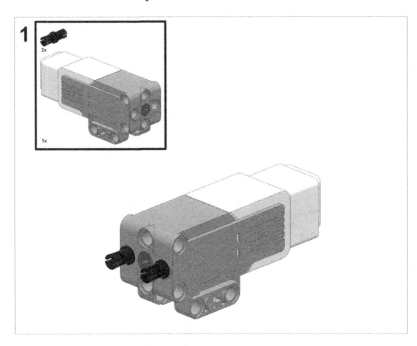

2. Next, attach the open frame to the motor. The open frame is essentially our gearbox.

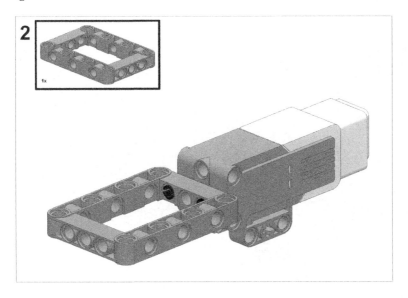

3. Next, place the 8-mod axle (with stop) and the beveled gear into the medium motor. Make sure the axle fits into the motor.

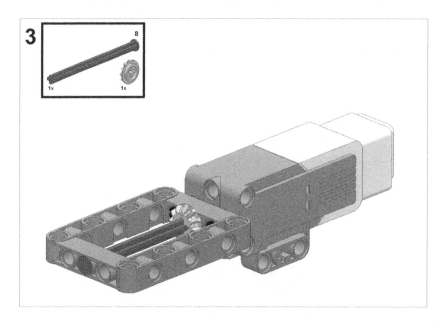

4. Now, insert the large gear and an axle into your gearbox. The teeth of both the gears should interlock.

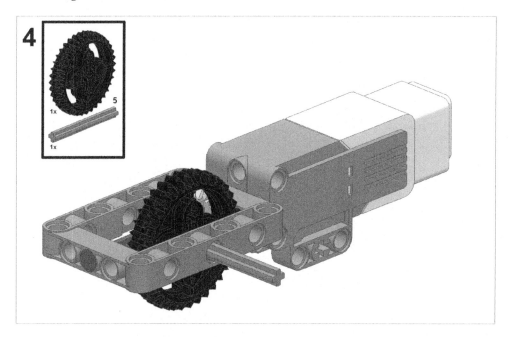

5. Finally, add a flag so you can see the rotations of the large gear.

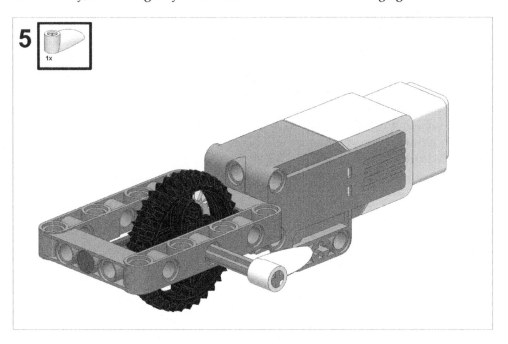

Next, write this simple program. The main differences from before are that now we are using the Medium Motor block instead of the Large Motor block and connecting it to port A rather than port D. On the Programming Palette, you will find the Medium Motor block just to the left of the Large Motor block. If we set the motor to rotate for four rotations, we will find that the large gear rotates slightly more than once. Although the flag is rotating slower, we have gained strength or increased our torque.

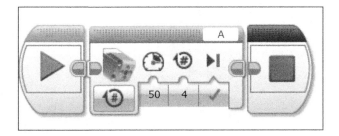

Worm gear

For our next model, we will build a gearbox that contains a worm gear. Every time the worm gear makes one complete rotation, the spur or straight gear meshed to it will progress by one tooth. We are using a 24-tooth spur gear in this model. Notice how this spur gear does not have any bevels. You will find that our spur gear will rotate very slowly, but we have a mechanical advantage of 24! Speed is not always the goal of a gearbox. Besides greater torque, one feature I like about using a worm gear is the greater amount of control. If you are building an arm where great precision is required, the worm gear will allow you to align your output appendage with a high degree of accuracy. The EV3 shaft encoders can guide the motors themselves to within one degree of accuracy. So with this combination of gears, we have an accuracy of 1/24 of a degree.

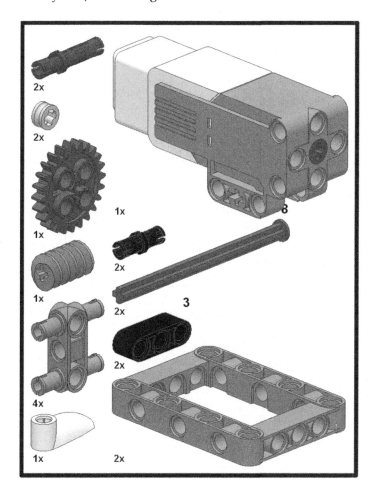

In the following seven steps, we will build the gearbox with a worm gear:

1. First insert two long friction pins into your medium motor. The short side of the pins should go into the motor.

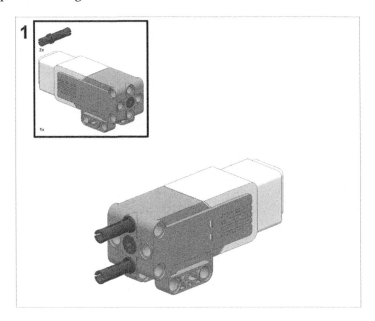

2. Next, add an open frame with two friction pins in the frame.

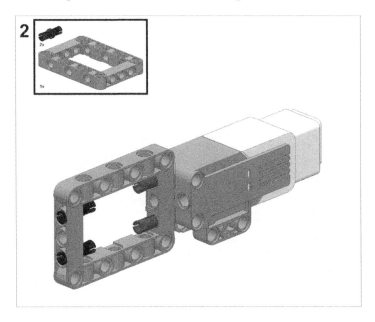

3. Now, add two 3-mod beams to the inside of the open frame. These beams will reinforce the axle and prevent the worm gear from sliding back and forth.

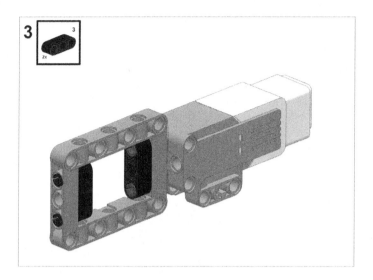

4. Now, add in an 8-mod stopped axle, the worm gear, and two half bushings. The axle should go all the way into the motor.

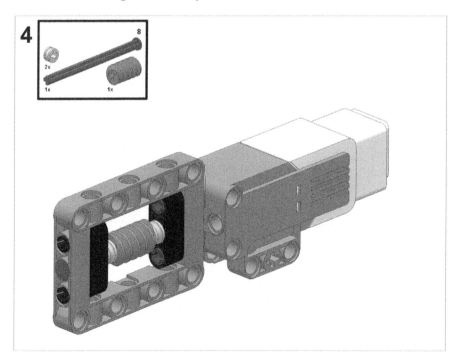

5. Now we will add some 3-mod perpendicular pin connectors to the open frame. This is creating support for the other half of our gearbox.

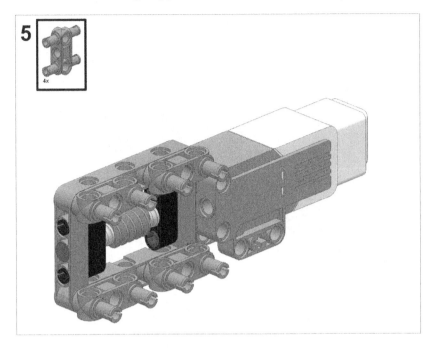

6. Now, add the second open frame along with the 24-tooth straight gear.

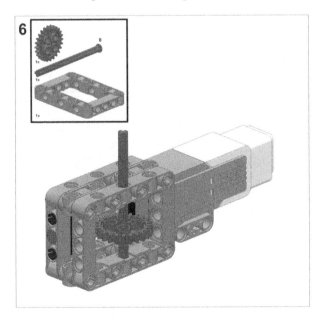

7. Now we will add the white flag so you can see the progress of the axle.

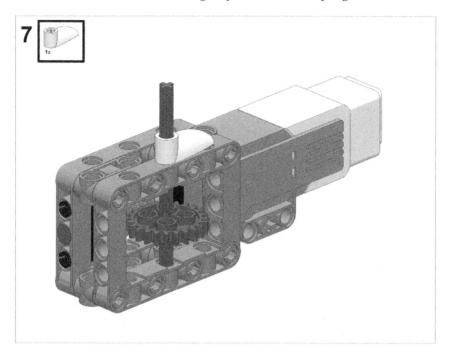

We can download a similar program to what you wrote for the beveled gear. Increase the number of rotations, as this gearbox will move slowly. Again, make sure that your motor is plugged into port A of your EV3 brick.

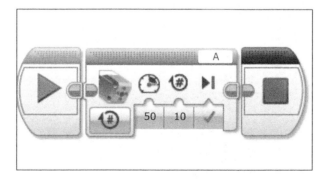

When you executed the preceding program, you saw how slowly the straight gear turned. It can be difficult to visualize how many times the worm gear has turned. We are now going to write a more complicated program that will allow us to display the number of rotations of the worm gear on the EV3 brick display.

Using wires and parallel threads

In the following screenshot, you can see that we can have parallel commands in our program. Our primary command will be to rotate the medium motor. You can decide how many turns to rotate your medium motor for. Although in our original program the blocks are connected by touching each other, you can also connect the blocks with wires as you would a real instrument. If you click on the Sequence Plug Exit of a block, a wired space between blocks will open up. You can drag this wire to the next command block, such as the Loop block we will add in a moment.

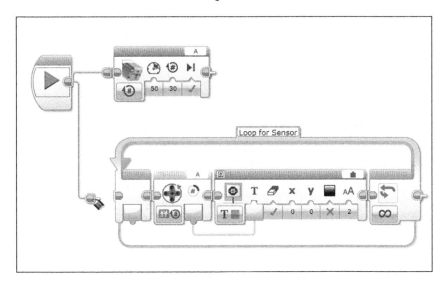

This also allows you to make your code two dimensional. One important aspect of visual programming is being able to view your entire code on the screen at one time. You can also split the wires to run parallel threads in your program. In this case, the wires run to both the Medium Motor block and the Loop block. When the program executes, both of these branches will run at the same time.

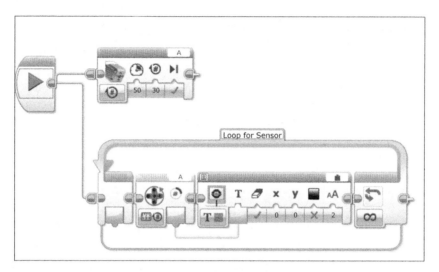

For your other parallel command, grab a Loop block from the Orange Flow Control tab of the Programming Palette. A Loop block continuously repeats itself and runs the command blocks that are inside the loop.

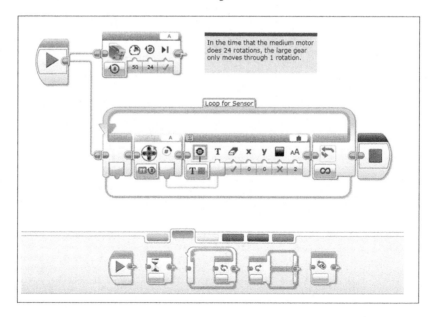

The following steps describe how to set up the blocks inside of the loop:

- Inside the loop, you want to put a Motor Rotation Sensor block from the Yellow Sensor tab of the Programming Palette.

- To the right of the Motor Rotation Sensor block put a Display block from the Green Action tab of the Programming Palette.

- On the Display block, you need to click on the tab on the left of the block to allow a text input from the Motor Sensor block.

- In the upper right-hand corner of the Display block, click on the Text Window — which now says MINDSTORMS — and switch it to Wired.

- You then draw a wire from the output of the Motor Rotation Sensor block to the text input of the Display block.

- Make sure that your Motor Sensor block has port A selected. The tab on the Motor Sensor block should have the number of rotations selected.

- On the Display block, you may also notice that the Eraser icon is selected. This will clear the display each time the loop is run.

When you run this program, you will see the number of rotations of the medium motor displayed on the screen. Since the bottom thread is an infinite loop, you will need to stop the program manually.

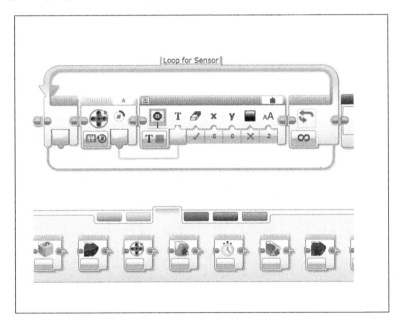

Summary

In this chapter, you learned how to use several types of gears included in the LEGO EV3 kit. We observed how to combine gears to increase speed or torque in a gearbox. We wrote simple programs with parallel threads, loops, motor feedback, and display output.

In the next chapter, we will attach two large motors to the EV3 brick to build a moveable robot.

3
Drive Train and Chassis

In this chapter, we will build a moveable robot. The robot will include a common chassis that will work with both the Home Edition and the Educational Edition of the EV3 kit. To keep these robots simple, I am not including gear reductions, but that would be a natural extension using what you learned in *Chapter 2*, *Mechanical Design*. All of these robots have a low center of mass, and a wide chassis, which makes it easy to use them for line tracking. The chassis will consist of:

- A frame
- The EV3 brick
- Motors

I will provide instructions for attaching different methods of locomotion to these chassis depending on your version of the EV3 kit. The robots include:

- Wheels
- Skids
- Caster ball
- Treads

Chassis

In this section, we will assemble the EV3 intelligent brick with several framing pieces and motors. You will be able to build several different models using this chassis by attaching additional LEGO beams and bricks. For the chassis, the only difference between the Retail Edition and Educational Edition will be the colors of the bricks.

If you have the Educational Edition of the EV3 kit, you will need the pieces shown in the following screenshot to build the chassis:

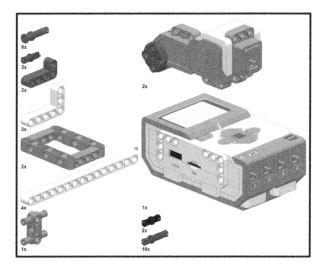

If you have the Retail Edition of the EV3 kit, you will instead need the pieces shown in the following screenshot. The only difference in the Bill of Materials for these two versions is the color of the beams. The Educational Edition has white beams with some red pieces. The Home Edition has black beams.

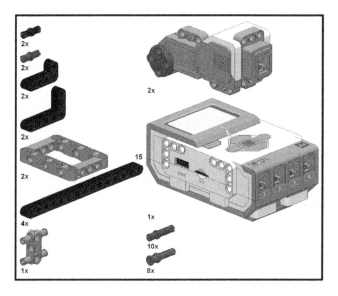

We will now build the chassis. The step-by-step build instructions I have included here are for the Educational Edition. First, take your EV3 brick and flip it over:

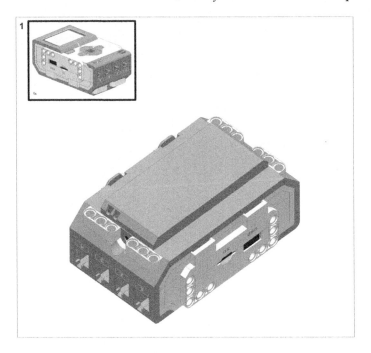

Next, we will insert four blue long friction pins into the EV3 brick:

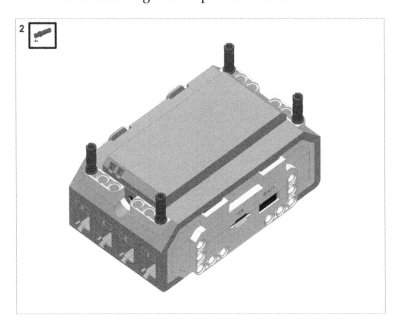

Now, we will attach the 15-mod beams to the brick. Remember, these beams will be black if you are using the Retail Edition of the kit and white in the Educational Edition.

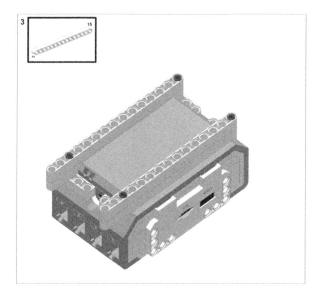

Now, insert four more long friction pins into the beams at the locations shown in the following screenshot:

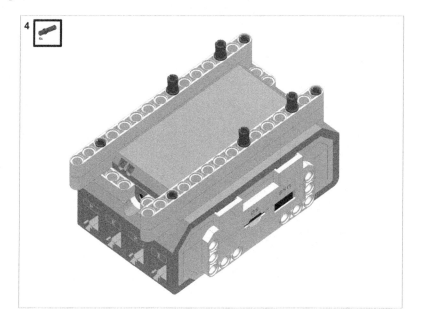

The following screenshot of the submodel is broken into three steps. This consists of the open frames we will use to hold the motors and some attachments.

For this submodel, you will need two of the 3 x 5 open frames and a four-pin parallel connector:

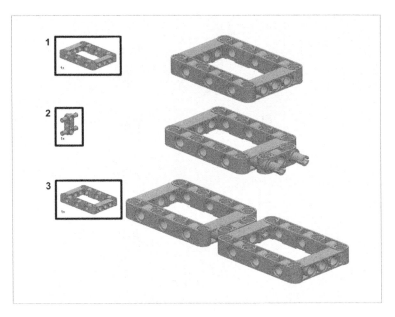

Now we will attach the submodel to the beams:

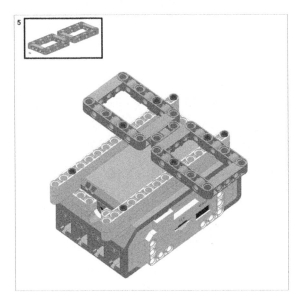

The next submodel will include the left motor and several pins and beams to allow us to attach the motor to the chassis. For the left motor assembly, you will need a large motor, a long blue friction pin, a blue-axle pin, a black-friction pin, a 3 x 5 bent beam, and a 2 x 4 bent beam. Note that the colors on the beams will differ for the Retail Edition of the kit.

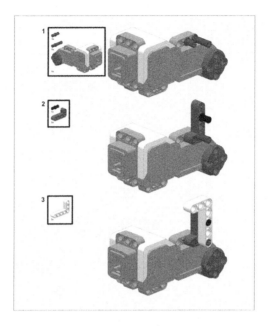

Now we will attach the left motor assembly to the chassis:

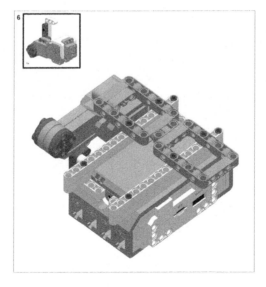

To hold the motor assembly in place, we will use two red stop-bushing pins. I like to use the stop-bushing pins because they are easier to remove and can prevent the assembly from falling apart. Things are inserted into the underside of the frame. Later we will reinforce the top of the motor assembly.

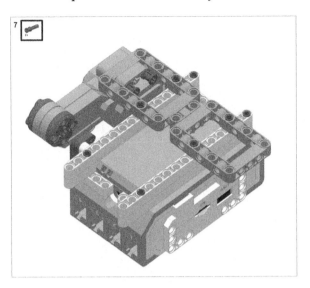

Now we will build the submodel consisting of the right motor assembly. This is identical to the left motor assembly except that the pieces are placed on the opposite side of the motor.

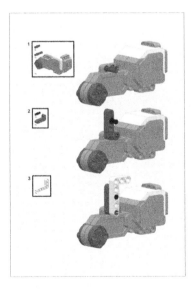

Once this is done, place the right motor assembly onto the chassis:

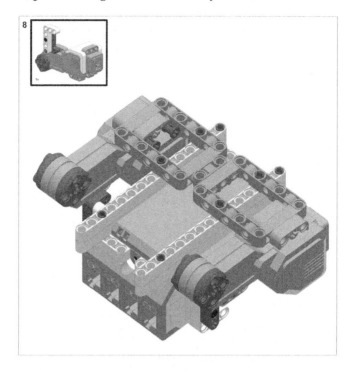

And as mentioned earlier, hold the motor assembly in place with the red stop bushings:

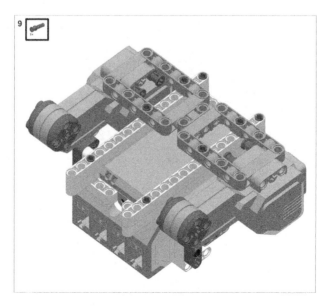

Now we will attach the top of both motor assemblies using red stop bushings. You will find that using the stop bushings will make it easier to take the chassis off if you need to change batteries.

If you are using the Retail kit, the shape of your final chassis will be identical but the color of some of the pieces will be different, as you can see in the following screenshot. This is the starting point for all four of the various robot models we will build in this chapter.

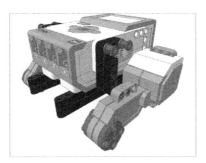

Next, we will attach wheels, skids, casters, or treads to our chassis. A robot with treads is more stable but often has a larger turning radius. The tread-based robot will also have a larger footprint. A robot with a skid or caster will turn better but only has three points of contact, and thus can tip easier.

Skid-bot with the Retail kit

The following robot uses two-drive wheels and a ski or skid plate in front. Although you can easily build a four-wheel robot, I find that it can be harder to maneuver a four-wheel robot with a high degree of precision. Depending on the balance of a four-wheel robot, the non-driving rubber wheels will provide a large amount of friction that will make it difficult to turn accurately and in a predictable and reproducible manner. Using a skid in the front reduces the amount of friction. In later chapters, we will do a lot of optical line tracking with our robot and for this I want a robot with high maneuverability; thus, we will build a skid-bot. The following steps are meant for the Retail Edition of the kit, but you can easily find pieces to build a skid-bot with the Educational Edition. You will use the following parts from the Bill of Materials in the following screenshot to assemble the skid-bot. If you have the Education Edition, you may want to skip ahead and build the caster-bot.

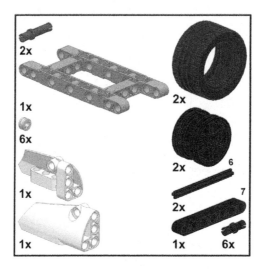

First, take your chassis and flip it upside down:

Next, insert four black friction pins into the open frames of the chassis as shown in the following screenshot:

Now you will add the longer open frame onto the chassis with two black-friction pins sticking out the front. This will make the level we want for line tracking.

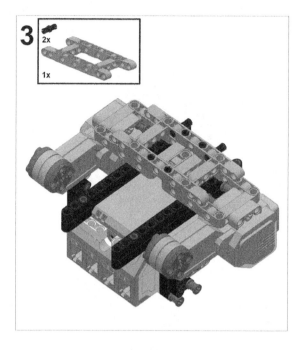

In the next submodel, we will assemble the skid. This consists of two of the white skid pieces interspaced with a black mod-7 beam. The beam will actually be on the centerline of the robot and is needed so that the robot is symmetrical and balanced.

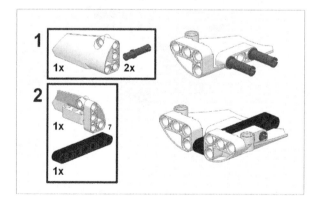

Next we will attach the skid assembly to our open-frame bricks:

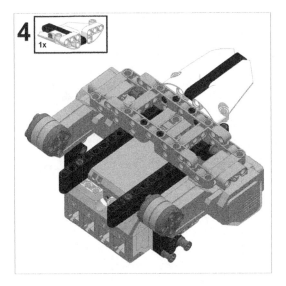

Now we will insert two 6-mod axles into the large motors to mount the drive wheels:

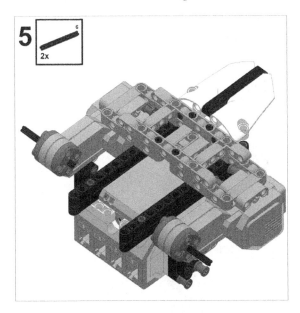

Then add four yellow half-bushings onto either side of the axles to prevent them from slipping:

In this step, we will add the hubs for the tires. Insert the hubs onto the axles in the orientation as shown in the following screenshot:

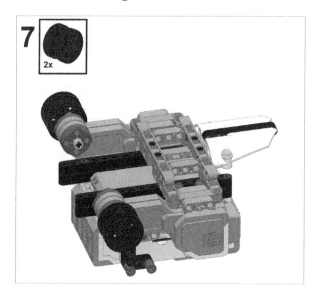

Next, insert two yellow half bushings into the hubs to prevent them from sliding off:

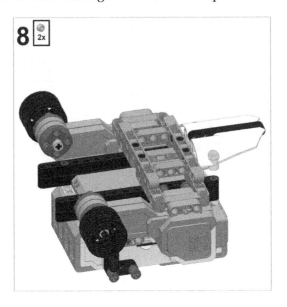

Finally, place the tires onto the hubs:

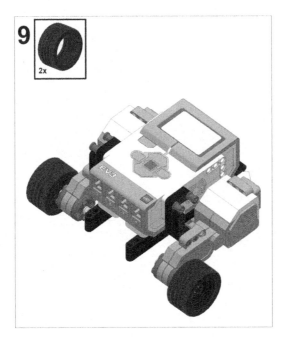

You will find that you could also build a skid-bot with the Educational Edition. However, because the Educational Edition has larger tires, you would have to account for this by adding an extra layer of beams above the skid so that the robot is leveled. As a warning, you will find that the skid will get scuffed up if you are driving on a rough surface. In the next three sections, I will explain how to build the caster-bot and two tread-bots. If you have just built the skid-bot, you may want to skip ahead to the programming section at the end of this chapter.

Caster-bot with the Educational kit

Although you can make a skid-bot with the Educational Edition of the EV3, the caster allows you even greater maneuverability because there is less friction. Having said that, the skid will actually respond better to bumps than the caster if your terrain is not perfectly flat. But I am interested in a robot that can be maneuvered with precision, so I am going to have us build a robot with the caster. Let's start out by gathering the parts seen in the Bill of Materials that is shown in the following screenshot:

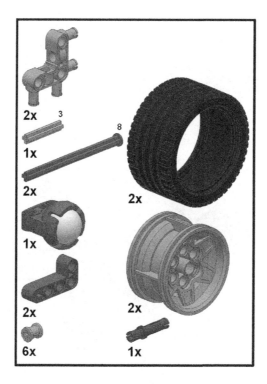

Start out by flipping over our chassis:

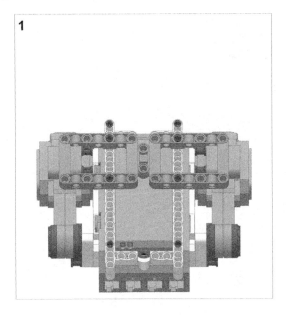

In our caster submodel, we will build an assembly to attach the caster to the chassis:

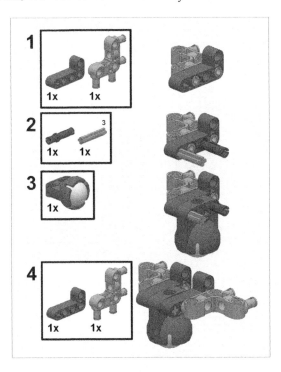

Next, we will attach the caster assembly to the chassis:

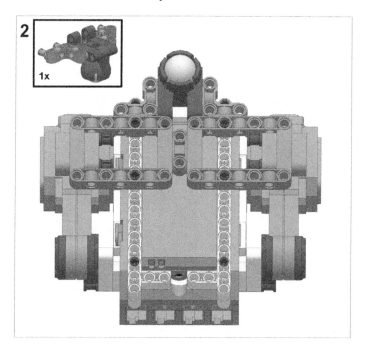

We now need axles to attach the drive wheels to the large motors. I am using the 8-mod stopped axles. The bushings are merely to provide extra space so that, as far as possible, the axles do not stick out of the robot and to prevent slippage.

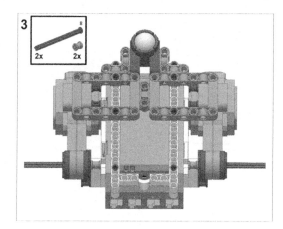

Now add bushings to the outside of the axles:

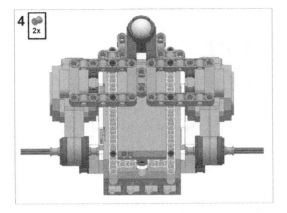

Next, let's add the hubs for the tires. Also, add two more bushings so that the hubs do not slide off the axles:

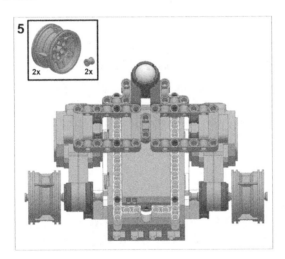

Finally, add your tires and the caster-bot is ready to roll! After you have added the tires, you can skip ahead to the programming section.

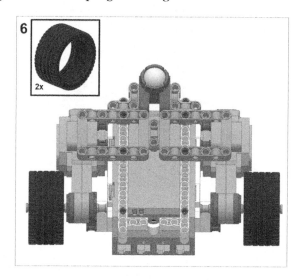

Tread-bot with the Retail kit

Tanks are fun to build and have the added advantage of easily climbing over obstacles. You will notice that a lot of tank designs will have larger center wheels. Having a larger center wheel can be particularly useful if you want to climb up ramps or go over bumps. Without the center wheel, if you are climbing over a bump, there is a chance of getting stuck. However, when you have a larger center wheel, your robot will often be tilted. Your robot will not be constantly parallel to the ground, which can be a problem with calibrating any sensors you might be using for navigation. I encourage you to play around with larger center wheels on your tanks, but the models I provide here have smaller center wheels. You will need the parts shown in the following screenshot in the Bill of Materials to assemble the tread-bot:

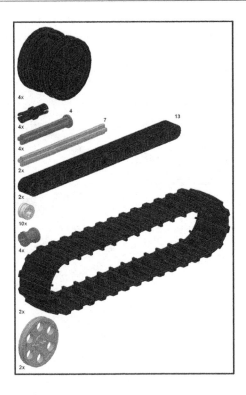

Start with your chassis:

You will now make two of the following submodels, which are the tread assemblies. You will start out by attaching pins, axles, and bushings to a 13-mod beam as shown in the following screenshot:

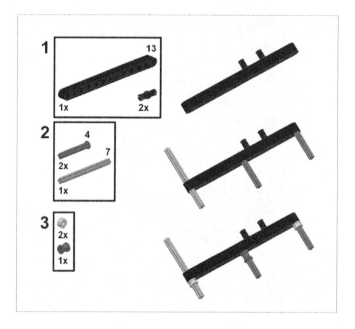

Next, attach the spoked black wheel hubs to the axles. You will secure the spoked wheel hubs onto the axles with the yellow half bushings. The gray tire hub is centered on the treads using the red bushings. If you were to add the rubber tire onto the tire hub, this would easily make the center of the tread slightly bigger. As it is, the bare tire hub lends just enough support so that the treads do not collapse.

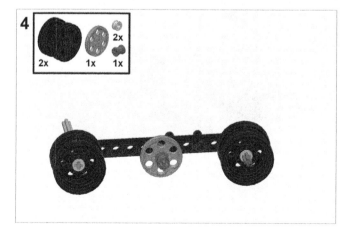

To finish the tread assembly, add the tread belt to each assembly:

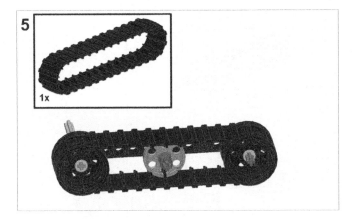

Now, add one tread assembly onto the right-hand side of the robot with the long axle inserted into the larger motor. You will notice that the black friction pins in the beam will insert into the side of the large motor:

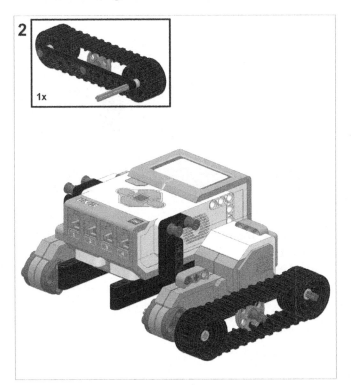

Now, add the other tread assembly onto the left-hand side of the robot with the axle into the large motor and the friction pins again into the side holes in the motor:

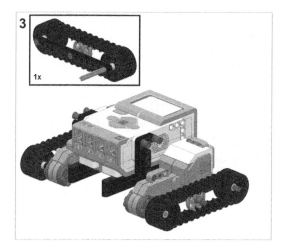

Finally, to prevent the treads from sliding, add two yellow half bushings onto the end of the axles that are sticking through the large motors.

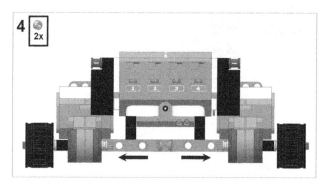

Although both the Retail Edition and the Educational Editions of the EV3 kit come with treads, you will find that the Retail Edition tread is a simple belt. This limits what you can do with the tread, but it does make it easy to use. The rubber does have more friction than a plastic tread, but only comes in one size.

Tread-bot with the Educational kit

Conversely, the treads with the Educational Edition of the Kit are multiple pieces that are linked together. Thus, you can make tank treads of different lengths. In addition to the hubs and pins seen in the Bill of Materials, you will need almost all of the links in your EV3 kit to make this tread-bot. For each tread assembly, you will need 26 links for a total of 52 links.

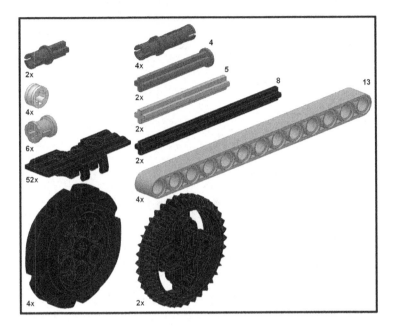

Start by flipping your chassis upside down:

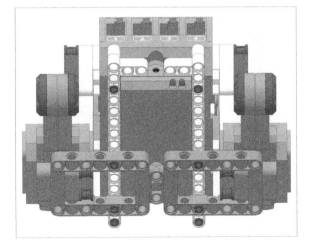

You will need to make two of the following submodels. You will need to build one tread assembly for each side of the robot. Insert axles and pins into the 13-mod beams and secure them into place using bushings, as shown in the following screenshot:

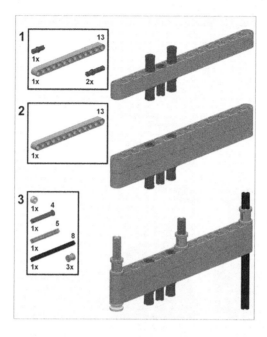

Next, attach the chain hubs to the outer axles and the double-bevel gear to the central axles. The gear is about the same size as the hubs, so the treads will be level.

To finish each submodel, add 26-tread links onto each tread assembly:

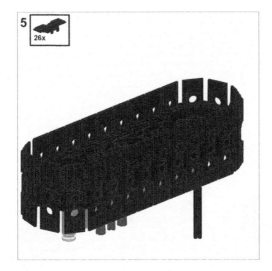

Now, you can attach the tread assemblies onto the chassis. The long axles fit into the large motors. The three blue pins will be inserted into the holes on the side of the motor.

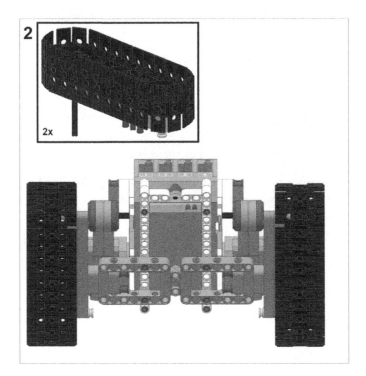

Finally, secure the tread assemblies into place by sliding two yellow half bushings onto the drive axles.

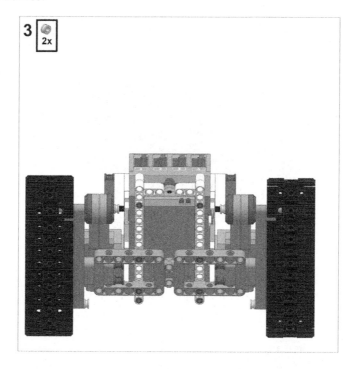

We are now ready to make our robots move.

Programming the robot to move forward

Before we program our robot, we need to attach the cables. Plug in cables from the motors into ports B and C on the EV3 intelligent brick.

Let's write a simple program to test out our robots. Drag a Move Steering block onto the Programming Canvas and place it next to the Start block, as shown in the following screenshot:

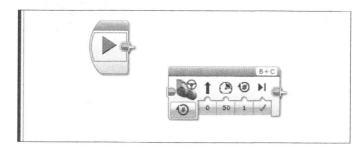

Using the drop-down menu, set the Move Steering block to **On for Rotations**. Set the number of rotations of the wheels to 5 as shown in the following screenshot. Remember that the motors have built-in shaft encoders that can tell how far they have rotated. The direction can be set to zero, which is straight ahead. The power level can be set to **50** percent. The motors are set to ports **B** and **C**. This is different from what we saw in *Chapter 2, Mechanical Design*, where the Large Motor block was only controlling one motor. The Move Steering block controls two motors at once, which is ideal for driving.

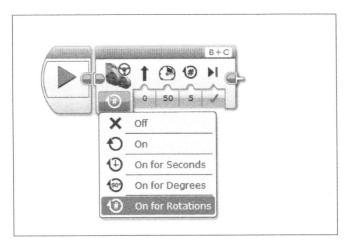

Although not required, you can end with a Stop block at the end of the program. Remember to make sure your robot is connected to your computer via the USB cable. Since our robot is going to be moving now, you might want to also connect via Bluetooth (we will explain this in detail in a later chapter). Next, click on the Download and Run button. Your robot should now move backward! You can also run it by clicking on the Start block.

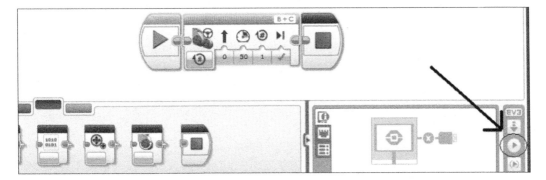

This chapter was heavy on mechanical design, so I will save the elaborate programming for the next chapter on *Sensors and Control*.

Summary

In this chapter, we used a single chassis to build four different types of robots. Using a common base will allow you to swap attachments and revise and improve your robot without starting from scratch each time.

In the next chapter, we will explore how to use sensors to make your robot interact with its environment.

4
Sensors and Control

In this chapter, we will have the robot respond to the environment using the sensors available in your kit. You will also take a reading from the sensor to display on both the EV3 brick and the computer screen. I will try to focus on information that is not already readily available in the EV3 help menus.

In this chapter, I will introduce:

- Programming blocks for sensors
- Official LEGO sensors such as:
    - Touch Sensors
    - Color Sensors
    - Motor rotation sensors
    - Gyro Sensors
    - Ultrasonic motion sensors
    - Infrared Sensors
- Third-party sensors such as:
    - Dexter industries
    - Mindsensors
    - HiTechnic
    - Tetrix
    - Matrix
    - Vernier

Using sensors

What is great about the official LEGO EV3 (and some NXT) sensors is that the software on the EV3 brick will Auto-ID the sensors as soon as they are plugged in. This makes it easy to use the sensors because you do not need to tell the brick what you plugged in. If you are using older LEGO sensors or sensors from other manufacturers, you will have to download and import sensor blocks that will control those sensors. The sensor blocks have the code to control the sensor and convert the signals from the sensor into readable values. You can download these .ev3b files from the manufacturer's website. These third-party companies include HiTechnic, Dexter, and Vernier to name a few. The Retail Home Edition and the Educational Edition of the EV3 kit come with different sensors. The Educational Edition of the software is ready to use all of the EV3 sensors. The Retail Home Edition of the software is not ready to use the gyro or the Ultrasonic motion sensor. To use the gyro or the Ultrasonic motion sensor, you will have to download the sensors blocks from LEGO. Later in this chapter, we will download and import these sensor blocks. But first we are going to learn how to use the sensors in your kit. We can use sensors to collect data or we can use them to allow the robot to react to the environment. In the Educational Edition of the software, we can collect large data sets from the sensors using the Data Logging features that we will explore in *Chapter 9, Experiment Software and Data Logging*.

Programming blocks

One thing that is confusing about the term "Sensor Block" is that it is used for both the downloadable .ev3b block file, and the icons you can find on the yellow tab of your Programming Palette, as shown in the following screenshot. An .ev3b block file can contain any kind of programming block, not just blocks for sensors.

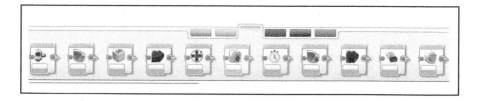

The preceding screenshot contains all the sensor blocks you can find in the Educational Edition of the software. The Home Edition does not include the Gyro and Ultrasonic Sensor blocks. The Home Edition does not have the legacy NXT sensor blocks such as the sound sensor, the temperature sensor, or the energy meter. We will show how to import these sensor blocks later in the chapter. You can drag any of the sensor blocks from the Sensor tab of the Programming Palette onto your Programming Canvas.

I will start by describing the simplest sensor block, which is the Touch Sensor block. Most sensors have a tab, called the Mode Selector that controls the output of the sensor block. In the following screenshot, I have clicked on the Control tab for the Touch Sensor block and asked it to measure the state of the Touch Sensor.

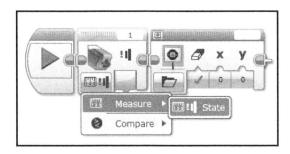

You can also drag a wire from the output socket of the sensor block to deliver data to another programming block. In the following screenshot, I am dragging a wire from the output socket of the Touch Sensor block to plug into a Display block:

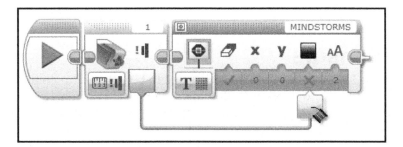

You can also use sensors to control the various flow control blocks that can be found on the orange tab of the Programming Palette. In the following screenshot, I have shown several flow control blocks that are all controlled by the Touch Sensor. The Flow Control blocks shown in the screenshot include a Wait block, a Loop, and a Case Structure.

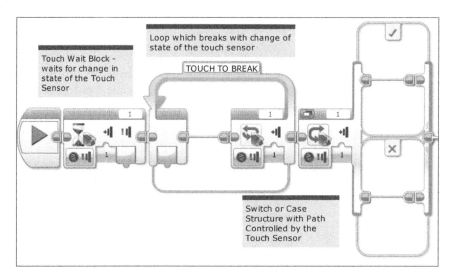

LEGO EV3 sensors

We are now going to try using all of the sensors. I will focus mostly on the Touch, Color, and rotation sensors, as those are common to both editions of the EV3 set.

Touch Sensors

Like most of the EV3 sensors, the Touch Sensor can be attached to your robot using either pins or axles as shown in the following screenshot. The Touch Sensor is a logic sensor with only two positions: on or off. Thus, the output of a Touch Sensor is either a 0 (for released) or 1 (for pressed). Although it is straightforward to press the red button to activate the Touch Sensor, you can mechanically extend its range by inserting an axle into the red button on the Touch Sensor, as shown in the screenshot. If you didn't want to attach the Touch Sensor to the robot directly, with a long cable the Touch Sensor could be used as a sort of tether control for your robot.

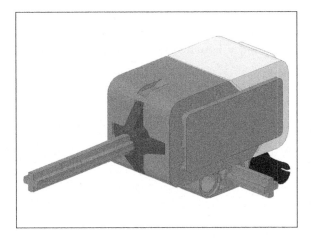

When you plug in the Touch Sensor into the EV3 brick, and the EV3 brick is in communication with the computer, the Touch Sensor will automatically show up in the Port View as shown in the following screenshot. The Port View is at the bottom of your screen to the right of the Programming Palette. In this case, the Touch Sensor is in port 1 of the Port View. Since the Touch Sensor is not pushed in, the number **0** is displayed right above the icon for the Touch Sensor.

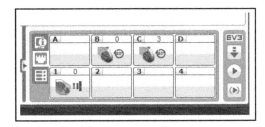

When the Touch Sensor is pushed in, you will read number **1** above the icon for the Touch Sensor, as shown in the following screenshot:

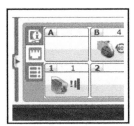

We will now write a simple code to display the output of the Touch Sensor onto the EV3 brick. We start out by dragging a Loop from the Orange Flow Control Palette. Inside the Loop, place a yellow Touch Sensor block and a Green Display block.

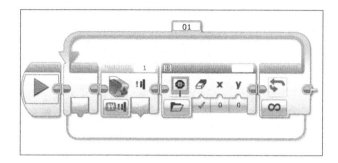

The default setting for the Display block is to read a file that will be discussed in *Chapter 6, Output from EV3*. By clicking on the Mode Selector for the Display block, we can switch from a file and navigate to **Display | Text | Pixels**. This allows us to display text.

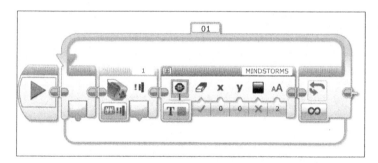

If you click on the Block Text Field (where it says **MINDSTORMS** in the preceding screenshot), you can choose a Wired input as shown in the following screenshot:

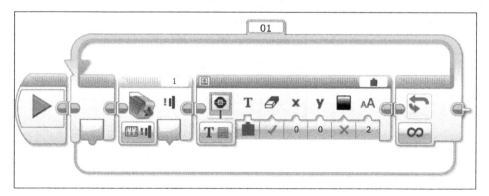

Next, drag a data wire from the output of the Touch Sensor block to the Text Input of the Display block. The Loop will allow the logic condition of the Touch Sensor to be continuously displayed on the EV3 brick screen. The output plug of the Touch Sensor block is triangular and the wire is green, which indicates that logic (0 or 1) information is being sent along the wire. Download and try out this program. You will see how the state of the Touch Sensor is updated on the screen of the EV3 brick. You should see a **0** or a **1** on the screen:

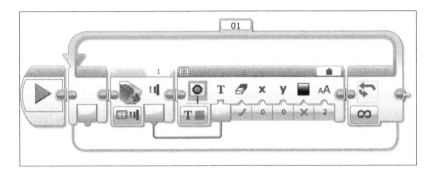

Now, let's use the Touch Sensor to control our robot. You can use any of the robots you have built so far with the Touch Sensor. In the program shown in the following screenshot, the first block is a Move Steering block with the Mode Selector set to **On**. This means that the robot will move until it receives another command. Then we drag a Wait block from the Flow Control Palette. By clicking on the Mode Selector tab on the Wait block, navigate to **Touch Sensor | Change | State**. This robot will move until the Touch Sensor has been pushed (or released, if the program starts with the Touch Sensor pushed in). Although in many cases you can ignore the End block at the end of a program, since we want the robot to stop we need to include an End block or a Motor block that tells the motors to stop. Download and run this program to control your robot with the Touch Sensor.

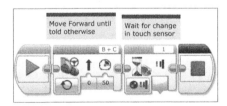

We will now look at some of the other sensors in your EV3 kit.

Color Sensors

The Color Sensor in your kit has three modes: color sensing, measuring the intensity of ambient light, and measuring the intensity of reflected light. The Color Sensor detects light with a photodiode.

If you want to use your robot to navigate and track lines on the floor, you will be using the reflection mode. In the reflection mode, light is emitted by a red LED. The photodiode in the Color Sensor measures the intensity of that reflected light. The intensity of the reflected light is particularly sensitive to the distance above the reflecting surface. The ideal height is about 5 millimeters above the surface. Light is emitted from the Color Sensor in a cone-shaped beam. Ideally, the intensity of the reflected light should be as bright as possible. If the sensor is too far away from the surface, the intensity of the reflected light will be less. The red LED in the Color Sensor will generate a circle of red light on the surface. The centers of the red LED and the photodiode are about 5 to 6 millimeters apart. In order for the detector to see the reflected light, the radius of your circle of light on the surface must be at least 5 mm. If the radius of the circle is more than 6 mm, then the Color Sensor is too far from the surface. If the radius is less than 5 mm, then the photodiode will not pick up the reflected light.

In the following screenshot, we show an easy-to-build attachment to hold your Color Sensor onto the front (or back) of the robot we started building in *Chapter 3, Drive Train and Chassis*. Depending on which model of the robot you build, you may need to add in some pieces so that the height of the sensor above the floor is about 5 mm. In *Chapter 7, Advanced Programming*, I will provide exact building instructions for a line tracker attachment for each of our four robot models.

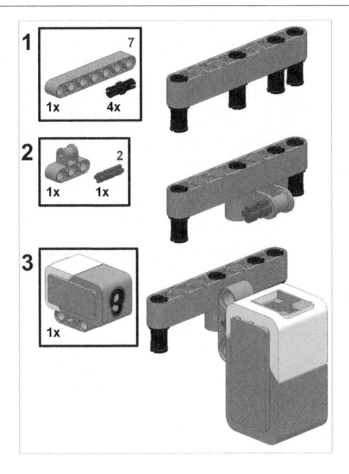

In the following screenshot, we can see the Port View for using our EV3 to measure color. Each color that the EV3 sensor measures is represented by a different number. We have the Color Sensor attached to port 4. The Color Sensor is returning a value of 5, which represents the color red.

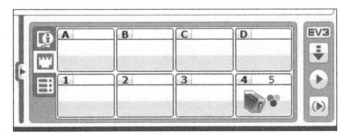

In the Port View, there are three choices of feedback you can receive from the Color Sensor: Color value, Reflected Light Intensity, and Ambient Light Intensity. When you first plug in a color sensor, the Port View will default to the Reflected Light Intensity. If you want to display the color that your sensor is measuring, you need to use the Color Sensing Mode. The EV3 will detect seven different colors, which is one more than the older NXT Color Sensor. However, you will find that certain third-party vendors have Color Sensors with an even wider range of detection. The number that you see in the Port View represents the color detected by the sensor. The following table lists the numeric color codes:

Color code	Color
0	No Color
1	Black
2	Blue
3	Green
4	Yellow
5	Red
6	White
7	Brown

You can use the following loop to display the color detected by the sensor onto your EV3 brick. In this case, the output plug of the Color Sensor block is a semicircle and a yellow wire passes a numerical data value to the Display block.

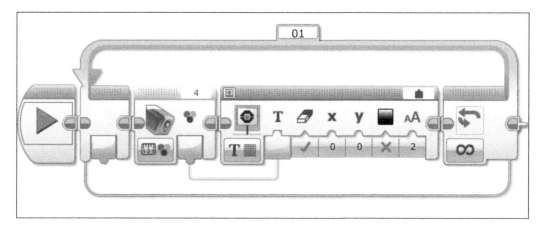

If you are just interested in finding out the overall intensity of light coming into the sensor, you can set the Color Sensor block to measure Ambient Light Intensity on a scale of 0 to 100. You will notice that, in the preceding screenshot, the Mode Selector of the Color Sensor block has three circles to indicate the Color Sensing mode, whereas the following screenshot has the radiating light symbol:

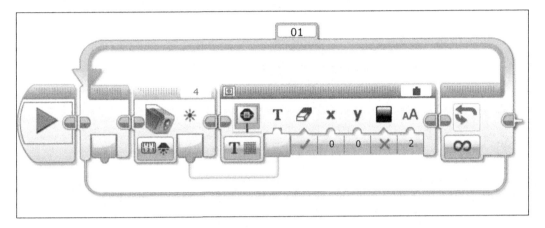

As mentioned earlier, if you want to use your color sensor for navigation, you want to detect the reflected intensity of the red LED. In the following screenshot, we have the reflected intensity displayed in the Port View:

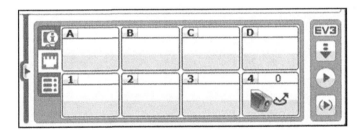

You can use the following program to display the reflected light intensity on your EV3 brick. Generally, white or bright surfaces will give a high sensor reading, and darker or black surfaces will give a low sensor reading.

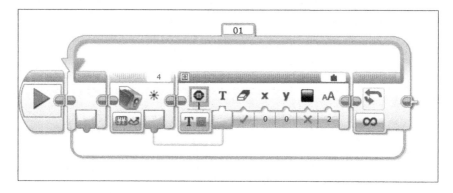

However, what you will find is that the intensity of the reflected light not only depends on the surface but is also highly dependent on environmental conditions. Your sensor will give different readings due to the ambient light in the room. This can create the need to *calibrate* your sensor and perhaps have cutoff bright and dark values. You could manually type in the maximum reflected values, but it is probably more worthwhile to test the ambient conditions. In this program, we use the brightest value detected by the sensor and send this to the calibration block:

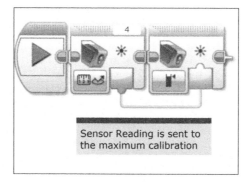

Sensor Reading is sent to the maximum calibration

The following program will allow your robot to move forward and stop when it sees a dark region. The Color Sensor block triggers at a Reflected Light Intensity reading of less than 40. However, you should read the reflected intensity of the darker region in your Port View to determine at what level to set the cutoff in your code.

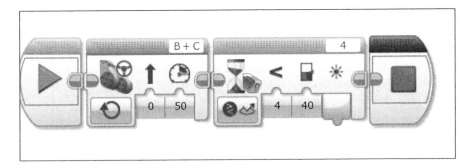

Motor Rotation sensors

Although not an explicit sensor, the motors have built in shaft encoders that tell you how far the motor has rotated in seconds, rotations, or in degrees. There is also a mode for the Motor Rotations sensor block that can found by navigating to **Measure | Current Power**. Some third-party motor sensors will allow you to measure the actual current. This can be useful if you are trying to determine at what point your motors are overpowered and will stall out. However, the EV3 motors are generous in this definition and are really just telling you the percentage (on a scale of 0 to 100) of the motor output.

The Degrees mode of your Motor Rotation sensor block is really useful for turning an arm or appendage on your robot. You can measure either relative changes in the position of a motor or the absolute position. However, if you are using the absolute position, it is a good idea to reset or initialize the Motor Rotation sensor. In the following screenshot, the Motor Rotation sensor is reset before taking a value:

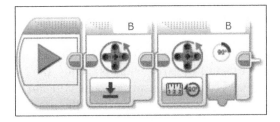

After you reset the Motor Rotation sensor, you can view the number of rotations in the Port View. You can physically push the robot or turn the wheels with your hand and see the following changes:

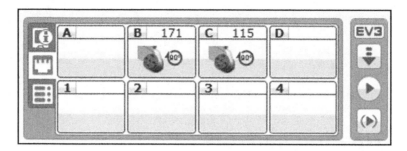

You may not want to constantly reset the Motor sensor. So this could be done at the beginning of your program, and the Motor Rotation sensor block can then go inside your Loop block. The following program will display the Motor Rotation sensor reading on the EV3 brick display:

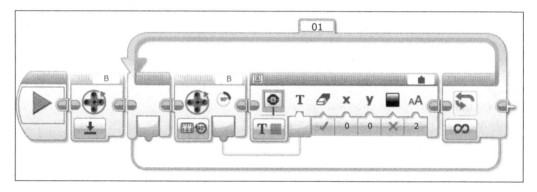

It is not always possible to navigate using lines on the floor (Light Sensors) or obstacles (Ultrasonic Motion and Infrared Sensors). Thus, the Motor Rotation sensors can be used to move forward by a certain amount. As you can see in the following code, there are several ways you could actually have the robot move forward a discrete amount. The Motor blocks have a mode controlled by the Motor Rotation sensors, from a programming standpoint, this is the most efficient way to move forward. Alternatively, you could have the Motor block set to **On** mode and wait for a signal from the Motor Rotation sensor block.

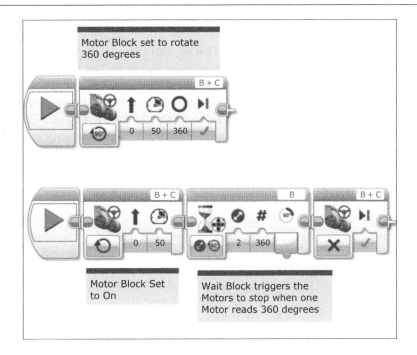

The process of changing direction using just the Motor Rotation sensors is called **dead reckoning**. However, keep in mind that turning a motor 30 degrees does not mean the robot turns 30 degrees. Only the motor shaft itself is turning 30 degrees. If you are not geared up or down, then the tire turns that same amount. To directly measure a change in angle of the robot, you would need to use a Gyro or a compass sensor. Although the Educational Edition of the EV3 kit does contain a Gyro Sensor, I know many FIRST LEGO League coaches who still insist on using dead reckoning or the position of the Motor Rotation sensors to navigate. You should remember to reset the rotation sensor if you are going to use dead reckoning. In the following program, the robot will move forward, turn a certain amount, move forward, and turn again:

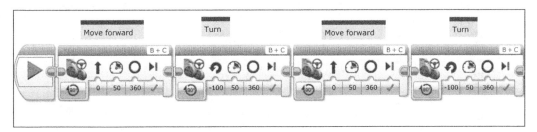

Navigating to a given destination can take a certain amount of trial and error. Alternatively, you can push your robot along your desired path while examining the output of the Motor Rotation sensors on the Port View.

Gyro Sensors

The development of new sensors by LEGO has been driven by strong demand and competition from numerous third-party sensor companies. The Gyro Sensor detects rotational motion on a single axis. You can use it to measure the angle (similar to a compass) or the angular speed. Using the Gyro Sensor will allow you to quickly make accurate turns. The Educational Edition of the EV3 kit contains a Gyro Sensor. There is a vigorous debate in the robotics community as to the quality of this sensor compared to some of the third-party vendors. Over time, I suspect the firmware to control the sensor will undergo substantial improvement. The Gyro Sensor will drift over time, so it is a good idea to reset the Gyro Sensor when using it in your programs. If the Gyro Sensor has any motion while it is being plugged in, the drift will be exacerbated. If the Gyro Sensor is drifting, the crude way to calibrate the Gyro Sensor is to unplug it manually and plug it back in while it is perfectly still. You can also calibrate the Gyro Sensor by using the mode selector in the Port View. Switching the Gyro Sensor from angle mode to rate mode and back to angle mode will calibrate the sensor. This can also be accomplished with programming, which we will demonstrate later.

If you bought the Home Edition of the EV3 MINDSTORMS kit, you can purchase a Gyro Sensor for about $30. If you have the Home Edition of the software and want to use a LEGO Gyro Sensor, you will need to download a sensor block or an `.ev3b` file. You can download the sensor blocks from the same LEGO web page where you initially downloaded the Home Edition of the EV3 software. You can download the Gyro Sensor block as shown in the following screenshot from `http://www.lego.com/mindstorms/downloads/`. If you have the Educational Edition of the software, you already have the Gyro Sensor block.

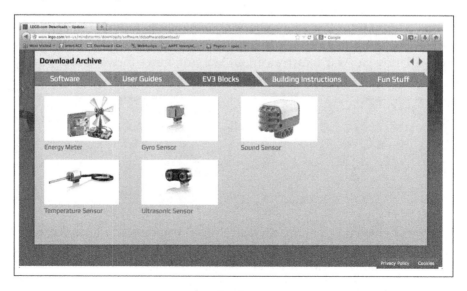

After you have downloaded the Gyro Sensor block, you will need to import the sensor block into your EV3 software, which you can do by navigating to **Tools | Block Import** from the main menu. The following screenshot shows how to import a sensor block:

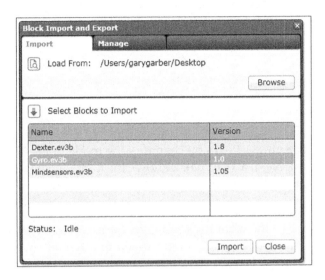

After you import the sensor block, you will need to restart the EV3 software. You will now find the Gyro Sensor block in the yellow sensor Programming Palette and the orange Flow Control Programming Palette. We are going to write a program to reset the Gyro and take sensor readings. For this program, I have a cable from the Gyro Sensor plugged into port 2 on the EV3 brick. Remember to keep the Gyro Sensor perfectly still when plugging it in. There is a mode on the Gyro Sensor block to reset the sensor to zero; this is the first block in this program:

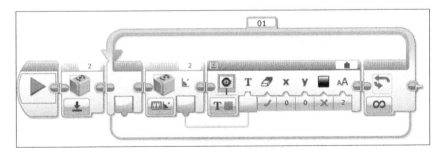

If the Gyro readings on your Port View are drifting, the Gyro Sensor needs to be calibrated by unplugging it or changing the mode in the Port View as mentioned earlier. You could also write a simple program to calibrate the Gyro Sensor.

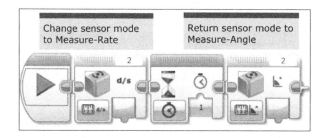

In the preceding program, we begin by changing the mode of the Gyro Sensor using the Gyro Sensor block. Next, a Wait block allows the Gyro Sensor the time to change modes. Finally, we change the Gyro Sensor back to angle mode using another Gyro Sensor block.

As I stated earlier, one of the main uses of a Gyro Sensor is to navigate. In the following short program, the robot is programmed to turn exactly 360 degrees or one full rotation.

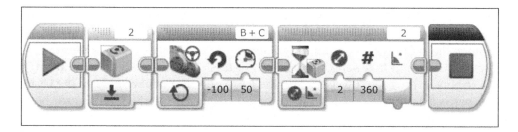

You will notice that, using this simple program, the robot does not make a perfect rotation. This is because you are asking the robot to stop exactly at the 360 degree signal, by which time it is too late because of the inertia of the robot. To account for this, we will have to use a more sophisticated algorithm such as a proportional control, which we will develop in later chapters.

Ultrasonic motion sensors

Ultrasonic motion sensors emit high-frequency sound waves (above the range of human hearing). The sensor measures the time delay between when the sound waves are emitted and when the waves reflected from an object are detected. If you have the Home Edition of the EV3 kit, you can buy the Ultrasonic motion sensor for about $30.

Similar to the Gyro Sensor, if you have the Home Edition of the software you will need to download and import the sensor block. There is a minimum distance that the sensor can detect from. If you are too close to the sensor, the reflections get blurry. According to my testing, the published specification that the range of the Ultrasonic Motion sensor is from 3 cm out to 250 cm is accurate. In the following program, we will display the reading of the motion sensor on the EV3 brick:

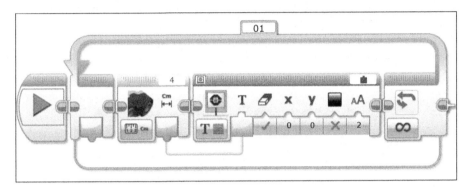

If you attach your Ultrasonic motion sensor to the front of your robot, you can use it to stop a certain distance from the wall. Although seemingly straightforward, in the following program I have included two parallel threads. The EV3 will display the motion sensor readings onto the display while moving. You will find that stopping at a discreet distance from a wall is difficult and that a proportional control is necessary to do this with precision. In this program, you do need the Stop block to halt the motors.

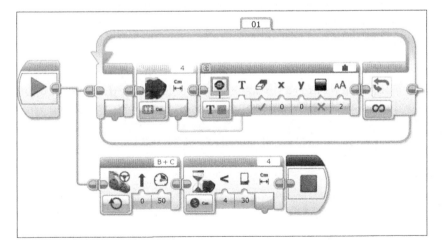

A new interesting feature of the Ultrasonic motion sensor is called **presence**. The intended use of this mode is to detect the presence of other ultrasonic sensors. This is important because if you have multiple ultrasonic sensors active at the same time, they interfere with each other. The older LEGO NXT Mindstorm kits had a sound sensor and presence can allow the robot to use the EV3 Ultrasonic motion sensor as a sound sensor. Presence is useful for detecting loud noises such as a clap. In the following program, the robot will move forward until it hears someone clap their hands. The Loop is broken by a change in sound intensity.

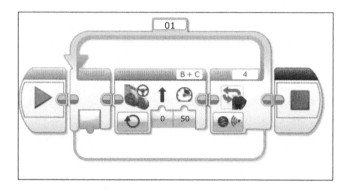

Infrared Sensors

Instead of the Gyro Sensor and the Ultrasonic motion sensor, the Home Edition of the EV3 kit contains the Infrared Sensor and the Infrared beacon. These will allow you to make both distance and directional heading measurements. The Infrared Sensor itself emits a cone of infrared light that can be used for distance or proximity measurements. The term "proximity" is used because the values returned by the sensor are not exact distances but give a relative distance based on the intensity of the reflected light. The proximity values range from 0 to 100 percent. For a bright object, a value of 100 percent is a distance of about 70 cm. In the following program, your robot will display the proximity measured on the EV3 brick screen while moving forward. The robot will stop when it gets to a proximity value of 20 percent. Remember to attach the sensor in the direction your robot is moving.

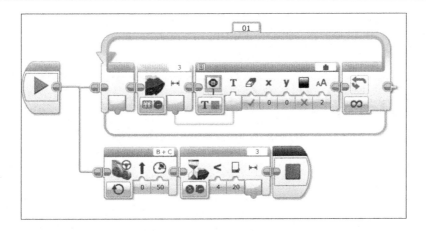

By itself, the Infrared Sensor cannot give directional information in the same way that the Gyro Sensor can. However, the Home Edition also includes a separate Infrared emitter, the IR beacon. The beacon has multiple channels, so you can use several beacons to triangulate your position as we will detail in *Chapter 8, Advanced Programming and Control*. For now, we will look at a sample code with a Wait block for a Beacon Heading block to allow the robot to turn to a heading based on the position of the Beacon. The range of values for the heading indication is from -25 to +25. These numbers do not directly correspond to degrees, but refer to different sectors relative to the front of the IR sensor. The following program will allow the robot to stop if it is approaching the desired heading from the left when it reaches a heading indicator of 5. Note that this will not work if the robot is approaching the desired heading from the right. We will need to develop a more complicated code using Math blocks to be able to stop from either direction; we will do this in a later chapter.

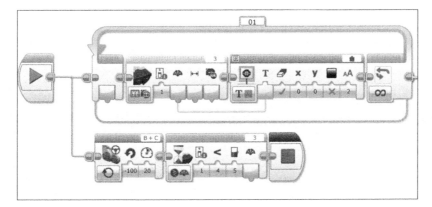

If you push buttons on the IR beacon, it can actually be used to communicate with the EV3 brick (similar to the remote control of your television set); we will discuss this in *Chapter 5, Interacting with EV3*.

Third-party sensors

As you go on to expand your EV3 inventory, look around at the multiple vendors that sell sensors for the EV3. Many of these vendors have been selling NXT sensors for years and are developing EV3 sensor blocks that you can download from their websites.

Remember, after you have downloaded the sensor block, you can import it by navigating to **Tools | Block Import**. Then select the sensor block you wish to import. In the following screenshot, I am importing the .ev3b file for Dexter Industries' sensors. This .ev3b file actually contains the sensor blocks for all of Dexter Industries' sensors.

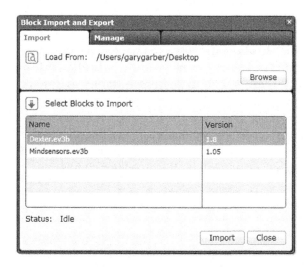

After importing the sensor block, you need to restart the EV3 MINDSTORMS software and your sensor will be ready to use.

Dexter Industries

Dexter Industries is a small company that makes LEGO sensors. The sensors are not enclosed and have the raw circuit boards with exposed electrical components. You actually connect pins and axles through holes in the circuit board. This gives an interesting look and makes your robot feel like less of a black box. However, this does make things fragile. Some of their coolest sensors include a GPS sensor and a 110 V relay for switching household appliances. They also have accelerometers and magnetic compasses. They have one `.ev3b` file that you can download and import into EV3 software and that contains all of their sensor blocks. The following image shows their **Thermal Infrared Sensor** and you can see the LEGO axles poking through the holes in the circuit board:

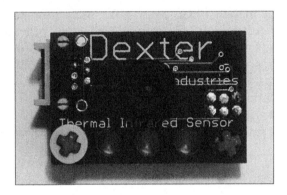

In the following image of the Dexter dPressure sensor you can see that it connects to the LEGO pneumatic tubes:

When you import their sensor block, all of their sensors will show up in the yellow sensor palette as you can see in the following screenshot. You can learn more about Dexter Industries at http://www.dexterindustries.com.

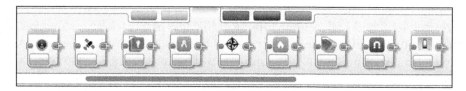

Mindsensors

Another small company making LEGO MINDSTORMS sensors is Mindsensors. One thing I like in particular about Mindsensors is that they provide sample code that shows you in detail how to use their sensors. Their sensors are similar to the other vendors but there are a few items I like in particular. First, they have a motor multiplexor that allows you to use more than 4 motors with one EV3 brick. My favorite item is the Sony PlayStation2 controller adapter, shown in the following image. Controlling your robot with a joystick is a major plus and one that is not built into the EV3. They give several programs that show how to use the PS2 controller.

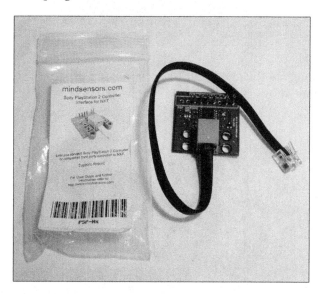

Similar to Dexter, here you can see the variety of sensors that Mindsensors offers in the yellow sensor palette. You can learn more about Mindsensors at http://mindsensors.com/.

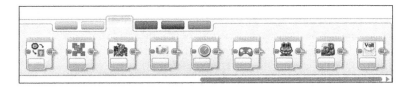

HiTechnic sensors

HiTechnic is the largest of the companies making sensors for LEGO and they have a formal relationship with LEGO. For several years, they were the main supplier of the electronics that would adapt the LEGO NXT to be used with high-end motors for the TETRIX platform, and the **FIRST Tech Challenge (FTC)** competition. In the following image, you can see an FTC robot my students built with a LEGO NXT brain that uses the HiTechnic motor controllers and sensors and metal TETRIX parts. Robots in **For Inspiration and Recognition of Science and Technology (FIRST)** competitions have numbers similar to race cars, as shown in the following image:

Most of the HiTechnic sensors look like older NXT type sensors and use actual LEGO NXT sensor cases. But what is inside the cases is a huge variety of sensors, including gyros, force sensors, accelerometers, compass sensors, and infrared sensors. At this time, not all of their sensors have the sensor blocks written to make them compatible with the EV3. In the following image, you can see several HiTechnic sensors:

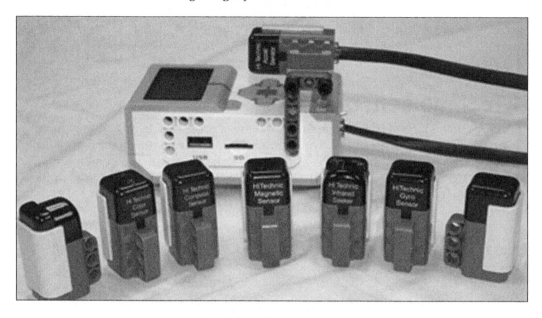

One of the most useful products HiTechnic has for the LEGO NXT MINDSTORMS are the multiplexors that allow you to use multiple sensors beyond the limit of the four sensor ports on a robot. At this point in time, they have not released the EV3 sensor blocks that will allow you to use them with the EV3. In the following image, you can see several ports for plugging in additional sensors:

If you want to build bigger, more powerful robots with the EV3, you need stronger motors as you can see in the following image. HiTechnic has been selling motor controllers that work with the NXT for years and they should release the Motor blocks for the EV3 software soon.

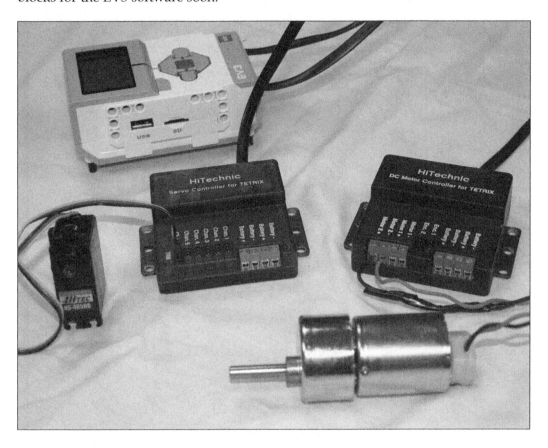

In the following image, you can see a LEGO NXT brick inside a metal TETRIX robot with HiTechnic motor controllers. To attach the metal TETRIX parts to your plastic LEGO bricks, you need special adapter pieces. You can learn more about HiTechnic at `http://www.hitechnic.com/` and TETRIX at `http://www.tetrixrobotics.com/`.

MATRIX motor controllers and metal parts

A less expensive alternative to TETRIX is MATRIX. However, the metal parts in MATRIX are of a thinner gauge than TETRIX and the motors are less powerful. MATRIX has released the EV3 motor blocks, so you can build a MATRIX robot with the EV3. In the following image, you can see an EV3 connected to a MATRIX motor controller hooked into a MATRIX motor and a servo. No special adapter pieces are needed to build with MATRIX because the holes in the metal are aligned, or on module with the spacing of the bumps and holes in LEGO bricks. You should note that the larger motors do need their own separate power supply and will not run off of the EV3 battery. You can learn more about MATRIX at http://matrixrobotics.com/.

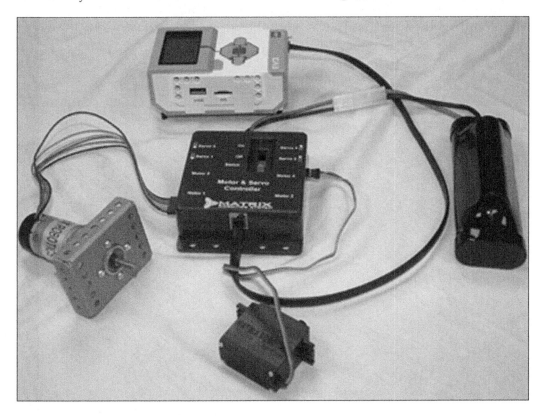

Vernier sensors

Vernier Software & Technology is a company that makes educational science hardware and software. Although they started as a company making data acquisition probes for the physics classroom, they now have a wide range of probes for chemistry, biology, and engineering. Most of Vernier's probes have **British Telecom Analog (BTA)** plugs on them. Vernier sells an NXT-BTA sensor adaptor that allows you to plug their probes into the EV3. In the following image, you can see a **Vernier Temperature Probe** plugged into an NXT-BTA sensor adaptor. As the adapter has been available for several years, it has the legacy NXT name. Vernier has a sensor block that allows you to use over a dozen of their probes with the EV3. You can currently use almost three dozen different probes with the NXT. Future updates of the Vernier sensor block will allow more of their sensors to be used with the EV3.

Although the probes are mostly useful for data acquisition, one could integrate this into a functional robot. The only area where you will find Vernier has probes that work with the EV3 that other companies do not is their chemistry and biology probes. They have a gas pressure sensor, thermometers, pH, salinity, soil moisture, and oxygen sensors. They actually have several types of temperature probes depending on your application. Their electrical probes will measure currents, conductivity, and voltages. Their optical and ultraviolet sensors respond to a wide range of intensities. One of my favorite sensors is their dual-range force sensor, which I have used in a wide range of physics experiments from measuring the force curves of model rocket engines to measuring the force your robot can pull with. The force sensor is also ideal for measuring how much torque your robot can exert in order to lift an object. In the following screenshot, you can see a sensor block that controls several Vernier sensors:

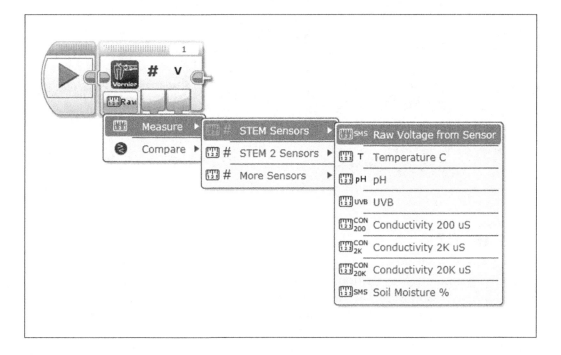

I have my students perform data logging with the EV3 and do gas law experiments such as Boyle's Law and Charles' Law, as you can see in the following image:

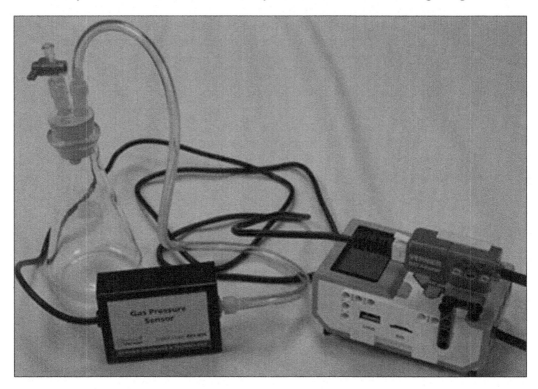

Summary

In this chapter, we learned about the different kinds of sensors you can use with the EV3. Common to both editions of the EV3 kit, we looked at the Touch Sensors, the Color Sensor, and Motor Rotation sensors. From the Educational Edition, we examined the Gyro Sensor and the Ultrasonic motion sensor. From the Home Edition, we learned about the Infrared Sensor and Beacon. We briefly looked at how to read sensors both on the computer and on the EV3 brick. We looked at sensors and motor controllers from Dexter Industries, Mindsensors, HiTechnic, MATRIX, and Vernier.

In the next chapter, we will examine how to control the EV3 using the buttons on the robot, and remotely using IR beacon, Wi-Fi, and Bluetooth.

5
Interacting with EV3

In this chapter, you will learn how to provide input to the robot. You will learn to interact with:

- The Brick Buttons on the EV3 intelligent brick
- The buttons on the Infrared Beacon
- Bluetooth control using a smartphone
- Wi-Fi communication

Push buttons

From the LEGO MINDSTORMS EV3 Help, you may be familiar with using Brick Buttons to start or stop an action. For instance, in the following program, the robot will move until a Brick Button is pushed.

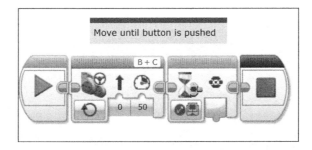

Using the Brick Buttons to enter information will take some advanced programming and involve variables, case structures, and loops. Using the Brick Buttons on the EV3 brick, we are going to select the value for the speed of the robot. We are going to write a program that has a Switch block and a Loop to select the speed.

The program will begin by prompting the user with text displayed to the EV3 brick screen. To control how fast the robot moves, we will use a variable called Speed. The program then enters a loop to register each press of the Brick Buttons. When the loop is terminated, the updated value of the variable will be sent to a motor command.

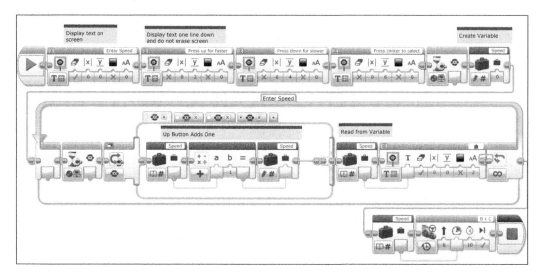

First, we need to display commands for the user on the EV3 screen. Most of the first row of this program is used to send text to the screen. You can only program one line of text at a time, so it will take four Display block commands to give the relevant information to the user. Notice that only the first Display block has the erase input checked and that the other Display blocks have the *y* inputs with greater values so that the wording does not overlap. In the following screenshot, we can see what the screen on your EV3 brick will look like when you run this program:

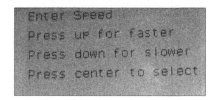

Next, there is a Brick Button Wait block followed by writing to a Variable block called Speed that we will set to 0. After defining the Speed Variable block, we create an Infinite Loop block called Enter Speed. This is an example of when knowing the title of the Loop block is important.

Later, we will write an interrupt for this Loop and call it by name. Inside the loop, there is a Switch block with four case structures that will be determined by the Brick Buttons.

When you create a Switch block, it defaults to two cases and you can add extras. This Switch block is going to allow us to increase or decrease the value of the Speed Variable block. In the following screenshot, the case structure is in the tabbed view. We will examine the case structure in the expanded or flat view in a moment.

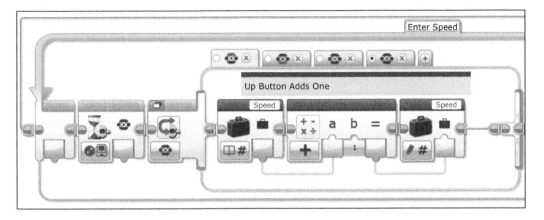

Before the Switch block, there is a Brick Button Wait block. This Wait block is waiting for a change of state of the buttons. Without this Wait block, when you press a button and continue to hold the button, the loop will run (and select the case of that button) for as long as the button is held. The initial Wait block allows you to only progress through the loop once every time the button is pushed. If you wanted to create an input where you would quickly scroll through numbers, you would not need this Wait block. As you can see in the following screenshot, after the Switch block, the value of the Variable block is displayed on the screen. A numerical data wire sends the value of the Speed Variable block to the text input plug of the Display block.

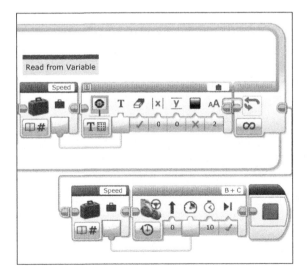

After the loop is terminated, the robot will move forward. In the preceding screenshot, we can see a data wire coming from the output of the Speed Variable block to the power input plug of a Motor block.

Now, let's revisit the case structure but with an expanded view. This will allow us to examine each of the four cases, as we can see in the following screenshot:

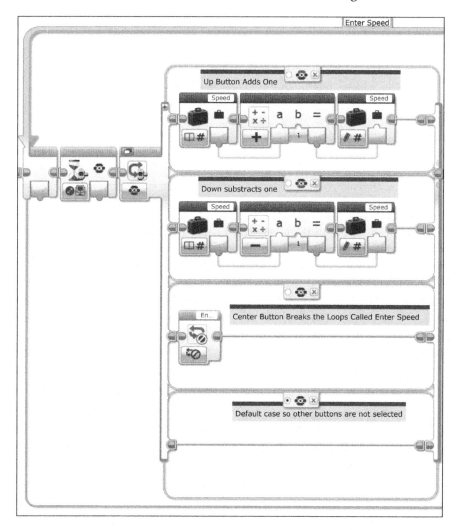

In the following points we will examine each of the four cases of this case structure or switch block.

- In the first case, selected by the up Brick Button, the Speed Variable block is read; the value 1 is added to it using a Math block, and the variable is re-written with this increased value.

- In the second case, selected by the down Brick Button, the Speed variable is read; the value 1 is subtracted from it, and the variable is re-written.

- The third case, chosen by the Center button, is responsible for breaking the loop. This contains a Loop Interrupt block that breaks the Loop called Enter Speed and moves the program past this Loop. This is an example of where the naming of a Loop is critical. The Loop Interrupt block calls the Loop to be interrupted by its name, as we can see in the following screenshot:

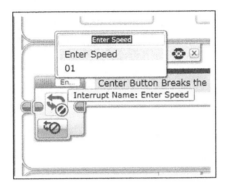

- Because the Switch is inside a loop, we actually need a default case that we do not plan to use. This case is intentionally a null operation, because we don't want something to happen every iteration of the loop. If we chose one of the other cases as the default, it would choose that case every other iteration of the loop.

IR remote buttons

The EV3 MINDSTORMS software Help provides good information on using the IR remote to control and send information to the robot. The following screenshot is an adapted version of what LEGO presents. Although the IR remote has only five buttons, the combination of buttons will allow you to send more commands than the Brick Buttons. Using different combinations of the IR remote buttons, the IR remote can send 11 different codes to brick; thus, you can actually have 11 different choices in a case structure.

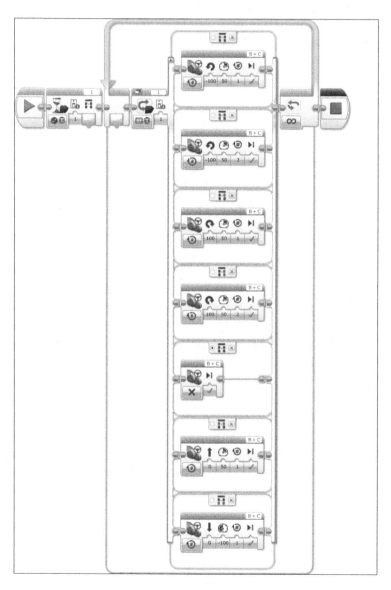

In the preceding screenshot, I have written a code with six different choices in addition to the default choice in the case structure.

Bluetooth control

It is well worth while to pair your programming computer with your EV3 brick. This will save the need to tether the brick each time you want to download your code. If you are working in an environment where there is more than one EV3 robot, you should assign a unique name to the robot. This can be done via the tether. If you have enabled Bluetooth on your computer, you need to make the connection from the EV3 brick. Next, you need to enable Bluetooth on the EV3 brick. In the following screenshot of the EV3 brick display screen, you need to select **Bluetooth** from the settings menu on the EV3 brick.

The Bluetooth menu has several options. Make sure you have checked both **Bluetooth** and **Visibility**, as you can see in the following screenshot. When controlling the robot via Bluetooth from your computer, you have to disable or uncheck the **iPhone/iPad/iPod** option selected on your EV3 Brick. After checking the appropriate boxes, if you click on **Connections**, you will be able to search for, and pair with, your computer.

 If you are still using Version 1.1.0 of the LEGO MINDSTORMS software, Bluetooth communication does not work with newer versions of Mac OS X.

You should also assign a passcode so that another user cannot accidentally take control of your robot. The default passcode is 1234.

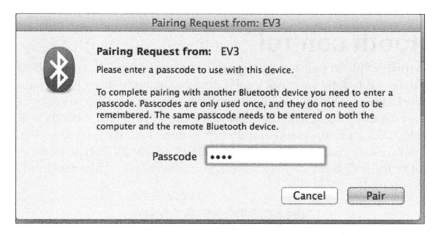

Keep in mind that the range of Bluetooth is limited. It gives you greater flexibility than having a tether cable, but not as much as using Wi-Fi.

Smart device control

Using your smartphone or a tablet app to control your robot is easy. There are numerous apps for the older NXT MINDSTORMS robot kits; over time there will be several for the EV3. The official LEGO app is called LEGO MINDSTORMS Robot Commander, and is available on Google Play for Android and on the Apple App Store for the iPhone and iPad. When pairing with your smart device, you need to make sure to select the special **iPhone/iPad/iPod** option on the Bluetooth setting on your EV3 brick.

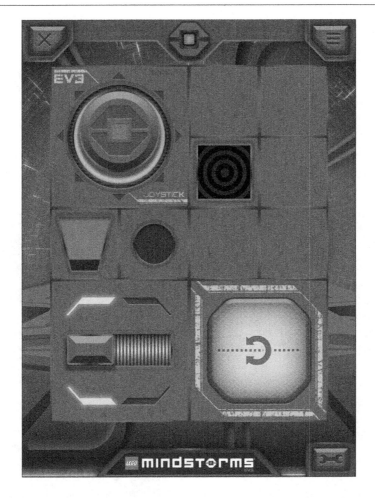

Robot Commander has controls ready to use for all of the robots from the Home Edition kit. However, you will want to create your own robot and controller. LEGO Commander will control assigned motors. You can create screen-based virtual joysticks, sliders, switches, or buttons. You can see the virtual joystick at the top left of the preceding screenshot. You can also use the accelerometers built into your smart device to control the robot's motors by tilting your smart device. LEGO Commander will allow you to take readings from the sensors available in the Home Edition, the Touch Sensor, the Color Sensor, and the Infrared Sensor. The bullseye in the preceding screenshot will light up when the Touch Sensor is pushed in. Instead of discrete numerical information, LEGO Commander will present a visual reading for the Color and IR Sensors. The brightness of the Color Sensor icon is proportional to the intensity the Color Sensor reads, as you can see in the circle below the joystick. The distance reading from the IR Sensor fills up the trapezoidal icon in the preceding screenshot.

Wi-Fi control

Although a highlight of the EV3 set over the older NXT is that it is advertised to be Wi-Fi capable, this is something of an exaggeration. There is a USB port that allows you to insert a Wi-Fi dongle. The current versions of the firmware do not allow compatibility with many dongles. The Wi-Fi dongle recommended by LEGO is the only one I could find that would actually work. Additionally, you will need to design your robot so the dongle does not protrude from your robot in an awkward way. In the following image, you can see that I have a Wi-Fi dongle resting just above the motor. You could also use an angled USB adaptor, so your dongle does not protrude out of the side of the robot.

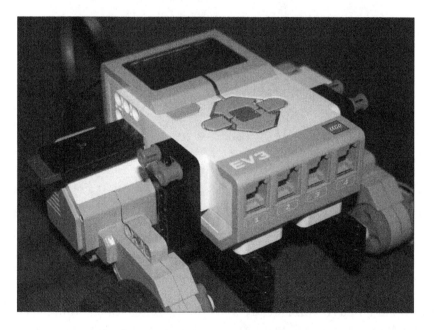

In addition to only a few choices for the Wi-Fi dongle, you need to make sure that you can successfully communicate with your router. In the preceding screenshot, you can see the Netgear WNA1100 dongle, sold by LEGO. For ease of use, you may want to set your router up without encryption or with WPA2 encryption. You should not have to enter the passcode directly onto the brick. If that is the case, you may need to change the encryption level on your wireless router. Even if your computer is on the network, you will still need to select the network through the EV3 software, as you can see in the following screenshot:

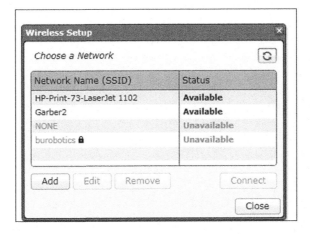

I found that, once properly set up, the speed of communication is faster than Bluetooth, but this is a significant factor only with large programs. The main benefit of using Wi-Fi is the increased range of communication. With Bluetooth, you are limited to several feet, whereas with Wi-Fi, you are only limited by the range of the network.

Summary

In this chapter, you learned how to control and communicate with the EV3 robot by several different means. We controlled the robot using Brick Buttons, the Infrared Beacon, and smart device apps. You also saw that you can communicate wirelessly with the EV3 brick from your computer with either Bluetooth or Wi-Fi.

In the next chapter, we will explore various forms of output from the robot, including sound, lights, and the display.

6
Output from EV3

In this chapter, we will explore how to send output from the EV3 brick. Output from the EV3 can be visual via the display screen, the built-in brick lights, or external lights. We will use the speaker to generate sounds. In this chapter, we will cover:

- How to display stock images
- How to use the Image Editor
- How to display your images
- How to display data
- Using the brick lights
- Powering non-EV3 LEGO lights
- Using the Sound Editor
- Playing sound files
- Making music

Display

In the previous chapter, we were introduced to the idea of displaying control values on the EV3 screen. This feedback is useful so you do not have to be connected to your computer to make changes to the way the program is executed.

After you have dragged a Display block onto your Programming Canvas, if you click on the upper right-hand corner on the File Name, you can load an image. As you can see in the following screenshot, the EV3 software has numerous stock images that you can use in the LEGO image files:

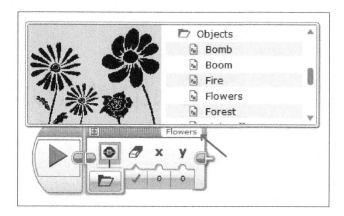

By clicking on the Display Preview button on the upper left-hand corner of the Display block, the display preview is opened. If the Display block is inside a loop or switch, the preview may get cut off. You can resize the loop or switch to make room for the display preview. The image in the display preview is pixelated. Although the EV3 software could generate a high-resolution image, the display preview is reflecting the actual lower resolution of the display on the EV3 brick.

Image Editor

The Image Editor is a great way to create visual messages to send to your user. The EV3 walks you through the basics of creating an image using the Image Editor. You can also import .jpg, .png, and .bmp images and edit them. If you are importing a color image, keep in mind that the image will be converted to a low-resolution black-and-white image. You can see in the following screenshot that the resolution of the Image Editor is pixelated, reflecting the lower resolution of the EV3 brick:

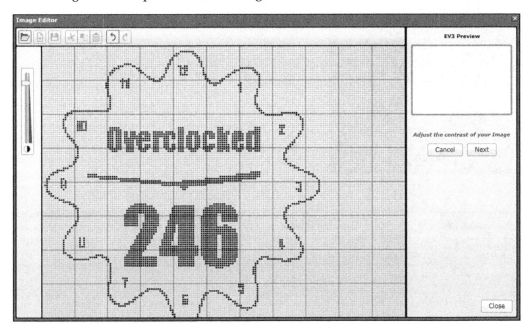

After you have created and saved your image, you can view what it will look like in your program before you display it on the EV3 brick. Similar to what we did earlier, by clicking on File Name in the upper right-hand corner of the Display block, you can load your image. If you are using the image you created with the Image Editor, it can be found in the Project Images folder.

You cannot transfer the images you have created between projects within the EV3 software. Thus, if you have created a great image that you want to use in multiple programs, you will need to export the image from the Project Properties menu, as you can see in the following screenshot:

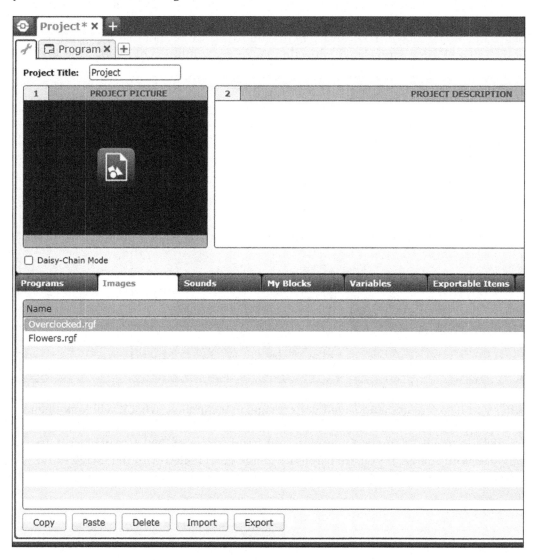

Display data

A very simple example of useful code would be to display a time counter on the screen. To do this, you wire the output from a Timer sensor block to the wired input of the Display block. You will want to erase the screen whenever the new time value is displayed.

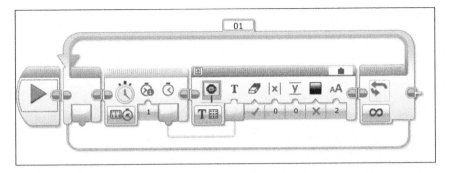

At the same time, you can display the value of a sensor on the same screen. In the following screenshot, the value for the Color Sensor will be displayed on the screen. You can choose the *x* and *y* coordinates of the text, and I have the sensor value displayed just below the time. Additionally, the screen is erased only during the first Display block. When you click on the Mode Selector for the Display block, there are actually two text modes, **Grid** and **Pixels**. In the following screenshot, I have used Text Grid and the program writes the sensor values to row 3 on the Display screen. Each row in the grid is actually 10 pixels high.

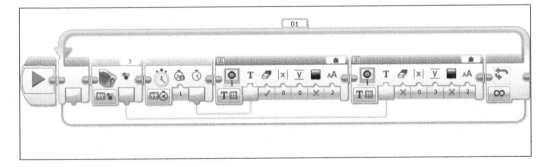

As you saw in *Chapter 5, Interacting with EV3*, we can also display the value of a variable. In the next program, I have added a parallel sequence where the screen displays the number of times a Touch Sensor has been pushed. There is a half-second delay in the loop so you can record discrete touches. This delay will prevent the program from adding to the value of the variable touches continuously while the Touch Sensor is pushed.

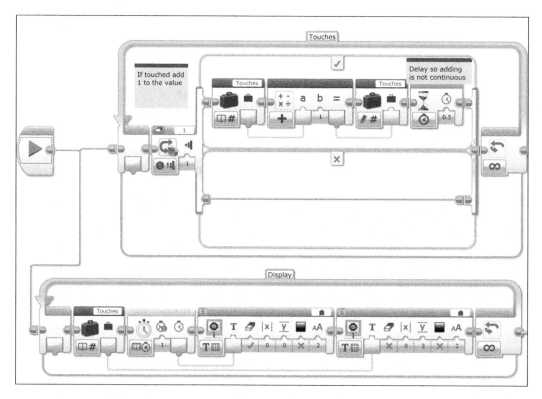

Brick lights

Brick lights are another useful way to provide visual feedback from your robot. Coordinating the color of the brick with other parts of your program can be interesting. In the following code, the color of the brick is dependent on the value of the Color Sensor. If the Color Sensor detects black, the brick will be orange. If the Color Sensor detects white, the brick will glow green. Otherwise, by default, if the sensor detects anything other than black or white, the brick will glow red, as shown in the following screenshot:

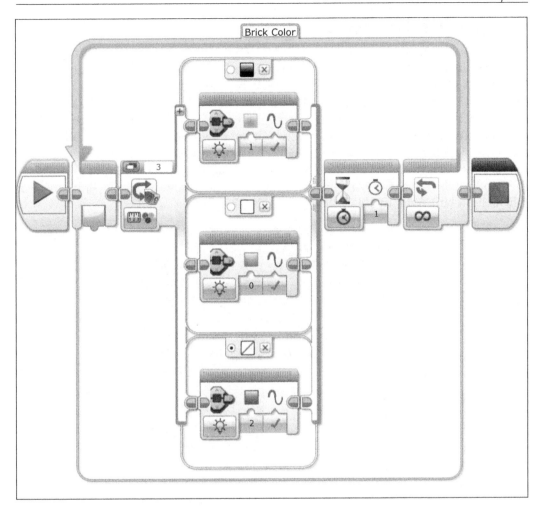

This allows for a cool-looking EV3 brick, and allows your robot to visually display information that can be seen from a distance. You may want to have lights that are not built into your EV3 brick. In order to use off-brick lights, you will need to use some of the legacy NXT MINDSTORMS parts.

Legacy NXT/RCX lights

Even before the NXT kit, the earlier RCX MINDSTORMS kit contained lights and a very simple motor that did not have a shaft encoder. To use these motors and lights with the NXT brick, you needed a converter cable. Because of the new Auto-ID system and digital motor control in the EV3, you are technically limited to using the brick lights. There are several solutions involving soldering and rewiring the cables with an extra resistor to allow older RCX motors, power function motors, and lights. The extra resistor would send a code to the Auto-ID system. To avoid soldering, you can use the black MINDSTORMS NXT converter cable to take the output from the EV3 and sends it to a two wire electrical signal. In the following image, you can see a LEGO light bulb from the NXT kit powered by the EV3:

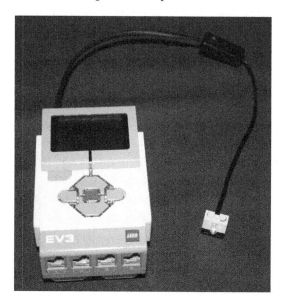

Even with the NXT converter cable, you will find that legacy motors and lights will not work with the EV3 brick because the EV3 is still searching for the Auto-ID signal. To avoid soldering and rewiring the cables, in the following screenshot is a simple program that you can use to power the lights (or RCX motors). The new control block here is the Unregulated Motor block. This block sends an electrical signal but does not wait for feedback from the Motor Rotation sensors, unlike the Large Motor block that would search for this feedback. We are not using the Unregulated Motor block as it was intended. If you controlled a normal EV3 motor, it would run continuously. By changing the motor power and inserting the changes into a Loop, we are tricking the EV3 into continuously powering an analog device. You can also do this with the older RCX motors. If we did not change the motor power setting from 100 to 99 (or any other value), the lights would only flicker for an instant.

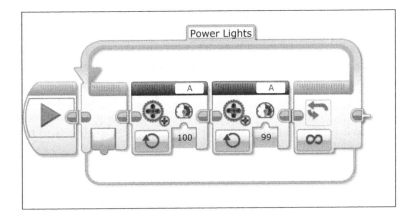

Sound

Using the microphone in your computer, it is very easy to use the Sound Editor to record sounds into a file to be used.

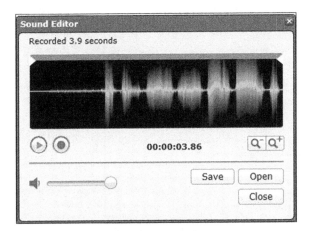

The stock sound files contain all of the system sounds and a variety of robotic noises. There are also recordings for all of the numeric digits. You could easily write a program for a countdown. In the following program, the speaker plays a **Count Down** using a combination of Switches (or case structures) and Loops. The loop runs five times, and the index of the loop chooses the path of the Switch. Since the index counter on the loop actually counts up, I used a Math block to allow the output to count down. Although I could have written this code using a linear sequence of blocks, I wanted to introduce another example of using a case structure to choose a sequence of commands.

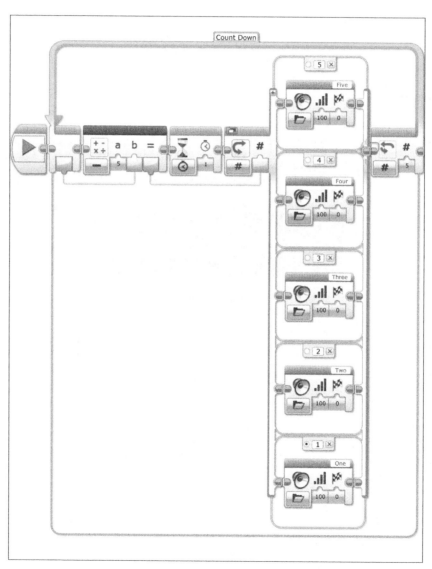

Music

With the Sound blocks, there are three modes. You can play the sound completely before moving onto the next block, play the sound once while the program runs the subsequent blocks, or play the sound repetitively while the program runs the subsequent blocks. If you choose the parallel modes, you will find that the sounds will only play as long as the program is running.

If you choose to use the musical tones of the Sound block, you have a choice between a musical note, or the actual physical frequency. By using the Tone mode, you can play a continuously changing frequency, whereas the Note mode is limited to the discrete values of the musical scale. In the following screenshot, the Loop first plays a continuous increase in frequency value where the input wire to the Sound block is a numeric value:

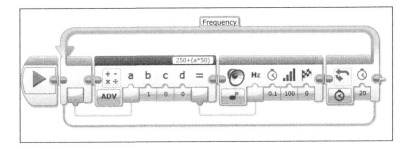

The range of frequencies the EV3 speaker can play starts at 250 Hz and peaks out at 10,000 Hz. In the preceding program, the other interesting block is the Advanced Math Mode of the Math block. You can program simple algebraic equations.

Summary

In this chapter, we explored various forms of output from the robot, including sound, lights, and, the display. You have learned about two of the tools in the EV3 software: the Image Editor and the Sound Editor.

In the next chapter, you will learn about advanced programming techniques, including data operations, My Blocks, variables, constants, arrays, loops, conditional statements, and case structures.

7
Advanced Programming

In this chapter, we will explore some more advanced algorithms with a focus on what we need for navigation. This will be particularly useful for programming your robot to navigate an obstacle course or play a complex game, such as FIRST Lego League. In this chapter, we will cover how to:

- Use Loops and Switches to drive in a square
- Use Loops and Switches to avoid an obstacle
- Navigate using Motor Rotation sensor feedback
- Navigate using Gyro Sensor feedback
- Simplify our program using My Blocks
- Simplify our program using Arrays

Using any of our four base robots, we will make the robot go forward, make a 90 degree turn, go forward, and repeat this sequence several times. In this chapter, I have included programs using both the Gyro Sensor and a process of navigation called dead reckoning. Dead reckoning, which is short for deduced reckoning, consists of calculating how far the wheels of your robot should turn by using the built-in shaft encoders (Motor Rotation sensors) on the wheels. For the dead reckoning programs, I used the skid-bot from *Chapter 3, Drive Train and Chassis*.

Loop and the Motor Rotation sensors

Let's start by using dead reckoning to drive in a square. As you can see in the following screenshot, we will first use a Loop block from the Flow Control palette and select the **Count** mode for the Loop block. We can have the robot repeat this turning sequence several times. Inside this loop, the Move Steering block will tell the robot to move forward for one rotation of the wheels. We will then have a Move Steering block that will turn the robot. Remember that a 500-degree turn of the motor shaft is *not* equivalent to a 500-degree turn of the entire robot.

This is a 500-degree turn of the motor shaft and the wheels, which I chose based on the design of the skid-bot. Depending on which robot design you chose to use, you will need to vary the value that the rotation sensor uses to trigger the stop of the turning motion to approximate a 90-degree turn. If you use any of the other robots from *Chapter 3, Drive Train and Chassis* (such as the caster-bot or the tread-bots) you will have to change the values for the rotation of the motor shaft. You could base this value on the diameter of the wheels you are using. Alternatively, you could determine the relationship between the distance and the turning of the wheel by using Port View and a ruler.

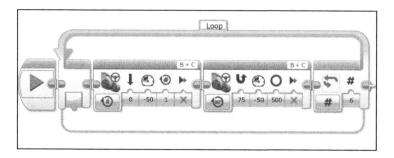

Try running this program. As you can see, it takes patience and some trial and error to get the robot to turn close to 90 degrees. Additionally, the amount that the robot turns can vary with the surface, especially when using treads. If you add several appendages to your robot, changing the center of mass of your robot can also affect how the robot turns.

Loop and the Gyro Sensor

Now we will repeat this exercise using the Gyro Sensor that comes with the Educational Version of the EV3 kit. If you have the Home version, you might consider buying the LEGO Gyro Sensor or the Gyro or Compass sensor from HiTechnic or other third-party vendors. You can buy the LEGO EV3 Gyro Sensor directly from LEGO, part number 45505, for about $30. In the following screenshot, you can see that the loop is the same except we will use a move to turn while steering until the Wait block is triggered by a change in state of the Gyro Sensor by 90 degrees:

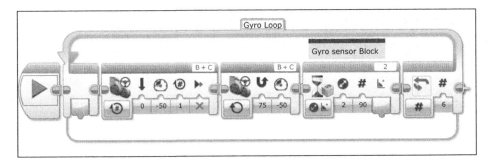

Before you run the program, you need to make sure the robot is absolutely still. It is critical to calibrate the Gyro Sensor. You can do this either by unplugging it and plugging it back in while the robot is stationary, or by changing the mode of the Gyro Sensor. You can change the mode using Port View or by writing this into your program. We can now run this program. If you notice that your Gyro values keep changing even though the robot is not moving, this means the gyro needs to be calibrated.

The Gyro Sensor detects rotational speed. You can use the EV3 software to calculate the angle or measure the angular speed. Using the Gyro Sensor will allow you to quickly make accurate turns. The Gyro will drift over time, so it is a good idea to reset the Gyro when using it in your programs. Including a Reset Gyro block and calibrating the Gyro Sensor are both good ideas when using the Gyro Sensor.

With both dead reckoning and the Gyro Sensor, you will notice that, using this simple code, the robot does not make a perfect square. This is because you are asking the robot to stop exactly at a discrete signal, by which time it is too late because of the inertia of the robot. In the remaining sections, we will optimize the motion of the robot and program the robot to steer around obstacles.

Troubleshooting with the Gyro Sensor

We want to diagnose why the robot is not turning in a perfect square. We will alter our program from the previous section by having the robot display on the screen what angle the sensor is currently reading, as you can see in the following screenshot:

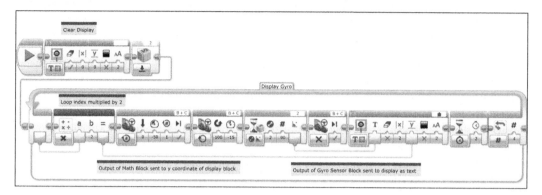

In the following steps, we will write a program to troubleshoot why the robot is not turning in a perfect square.

1. Before the Loop, clear the EV3 display screen with a Display block.

2. Set the Display block to **Text** and replace the word **Mindstorms** with an empty space.

3. Follow the Display block with a reset Gyro block to nullify the Gyro Sensor.

4. Reduce the number of iterations of the Loop block to 4 iterations.

5. Inside the Loop, add a Move block set to stop after the Wait for the Gyro block.

6. Place a Display block set to Text Grid mode with the erase input unchecked.

7. Add a Wait block (for 2 seconds) to allow you time to read the angle.

8. Draw a wire from the angle output plug of the Wait Gyro block to the text input plug of the Display block. Although the Wait block executes upon changes in 90 degrees, the output plug will send the value of the angle measurement after it has stopped. If you were to execute the program now, you would find that the displayed text would overlap. We can control the placement of text on the screen using the index counter of our loop.

9. Create a Math block at the beginning of the loop that will multiply numbers by 2.

10. Run a wire from the Loop index to the Math block.

11. Run a wire from the output of the Math block to the **Y** coordinate input of the Display block.

As the loop runs through subsequent iterations, the index increases and so will the placement of text on the display screen.

When you look at the numbers on the brick display, you will find that on each turn, the robot may be overshooting the turn. This is because the robot does not begin stopping until it reaches 90 degrees. And as it overshoots each turn, these errors build on each other to create a path that is anything but a perfect square.

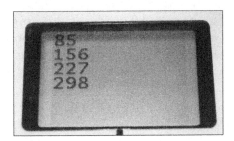

One challenge in using dead reckoning is to figure out the relationship between the change to rotation of the wheels and the change in rotation of the robot itself. Now, let's examine a similar program using the Motor Rotation sensor of one of the drive motors. It is better to measure the quantity of rotations for the motor on the outside of the turn since this motor undergoes a larger number of rotations. The Motor Rotation sensor has been reset at the beginning of the program. The Wait for sensor block uses the Motor Rotation sensor instead of the Gyro Sensor. The Move block does not have an output plug from the rotation sensor, so we had to use the output plug of Wait for the sensor block.

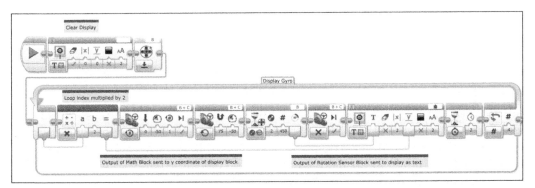

Of course, if your robot is connected to your computer via Bluetooth or Wi-Fi, you could read the value of the rotation sensor on the Port View of your computer. It is also a useful technique in using dead reckoning to have the robot move forward in a straight line to determine the change in the rotation sensor reading.

Switch or two-level controller

We will now use a case structure to add a correction to the turns. In the EV3 language, a case structure or if...then...else statement is called a Switch block. The Switch can be controlled by sensors and other logic statements. Although you typically will have only two cases, you could add several other branches to the case structure. Each branch of the Switch is called a case statement and can contain several programming blocks. We will use the Gyro and rotation sensors to define the case to try and "zigzag" onto the exact 90-degree angle to produce a square. In the following screenshot, you can see the entire code. As this program is extensive, it is worth noting how the wires are used to organize the code into rows, so you can see the entire program on one screen at the same time:

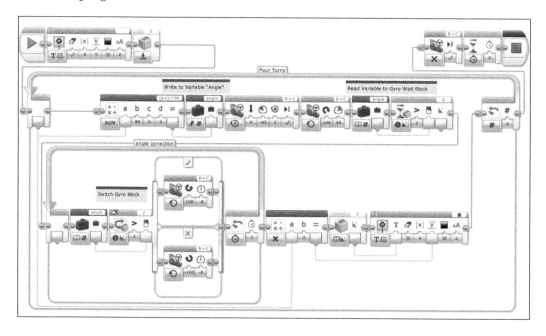

Initially, we asked the Gyro Sensor to only wait until it turned 90 degrees on each leg of our square. Now we will adjust our code to ask the robot to stop turning when it reaches, 90, 180, 270, and 360 degrees. We will do this using a Variable block set to write numeric mode. We will give this Variable block the name Angle. The index counter on the loop runs through the sequence 0, 1, 2, and 3. We will use two math functions to come up with these degrees. Run a wire from the Index Counter to a Math block set to math mode and add 1 to each number. The output of the add Math block should go to a Math block set to multiply mode. This number should be multiplied by 90 and the output sent to the Variable block. After the Move Steering block, the Wait Gyro block will be triggered when the sensor reads an angle greater than the Variable block.

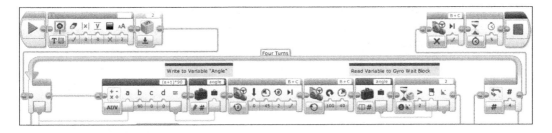

This brings us to the Switch block. The Switch block will have two cases defined by readings from the Gyro Sensor. If the Gyro Sensor has a reading greater than the output of the Variable block, it will follow the true case, which contains a Move Steering block set to the left. If the Gyro Sensor has a reading less than or equal to the output of the Variable block, it will follow the false case, which contains a Move Steering block that is set to the right. We will allow this correction to repeat itself several times by placing it inside a Loop block that will repeat the decision making for two seconds. The result will be a zigzag motion centered around the exact angle.

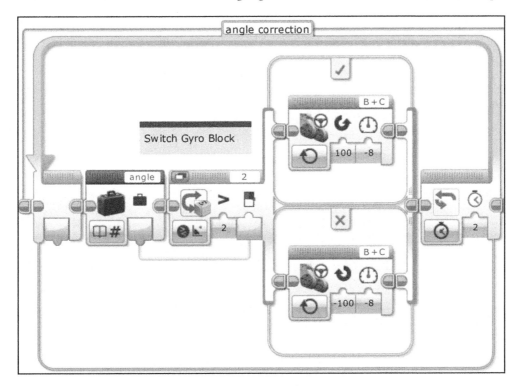

The preceding screenshot has an expanded or flat view showing both cases of the switch. You can also use a tabbed view of the switch, as shown in the following screenshot that shows the true case:

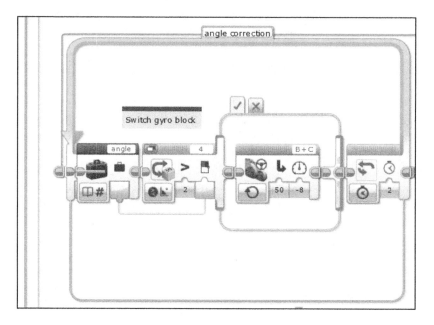

The following screenshot shows the false case of the switch:

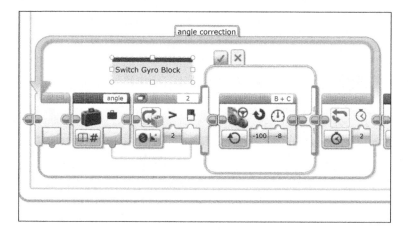

In the preceding program, we used a two-level controller with a logic switch. We hope to go as straight as possible, but because we a using a relatively weak algorithm for controlling the robot's turns, we end up with a chaotic zigzag motion. It would be more effective to use a proportional algorithm that would slow the robot down as it approaches 90 degrees. We will explore proportional algorithms in *Chapter 8, Advanced Programming and Control*.

Three-level controller

Now, let's examine a version of this program using the rotation sensor. This program is similar to the previous program except that the angle is set to 400 (the probable rotation of the wheels) and the blocks are set to the rotation sensors instead of the Gyro Sensors. The Gyro program used a two-level controller. A path in the case structure was chosen based on the robot's position relative to a setpoint value. Notice that, in this program, I have a switch within a switch. This allows for a three-level controller. When the robot is actually at the set-point value, no motion takes place.

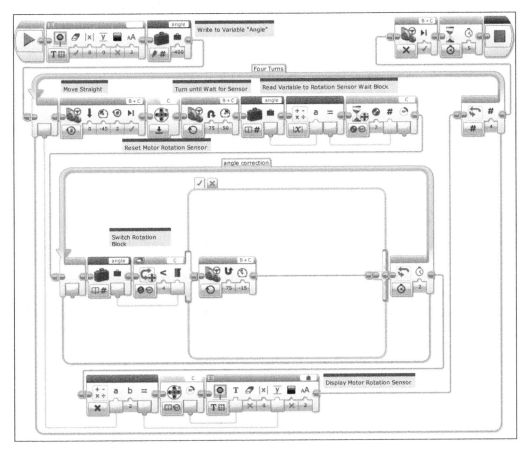

In the preceding screenshot, you can see the path the switch takes for the true case of when the Motor Rotation sensor is greater than the value of the angle variable. In the following screenshot, you can see the false case, when the value is not greater than the value of the angle variable. You can see in the screenshot that to make three levels we need the switch within a switch. In the embedded switch, if the value of the rotation sensor is less than the value of the angle variable, the robot turns the other way. For the false case of the embedded switch, the Motor Rotation sensor must be equal to the value of the angle variable. The robot does not move and we use a Loop Interrupt block to end the Loop. For the Loop Interrupt block, we must name the Loop that you want to end.

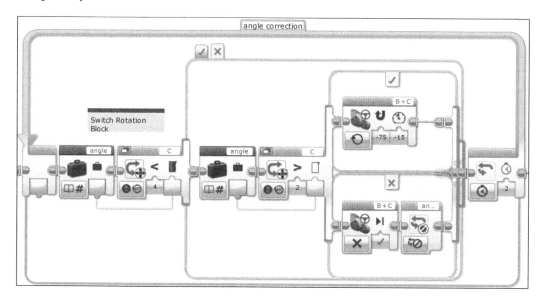

Subroutines or My Blocks

In this section, we will program the robot to move forward until it encounters an unknown obstacle with the Touch Sensor and then attempt to steer around the obstacle. An obstacle such as a table or chair leg would be ideal. We will program the robot to take input from the brick buttons. The program we will initially write is inefficient and repetitive. It is actually a good example of how you shouldn't write a program. We will first simplify the code using the EV3 version of a subroutine or function that is called My Block. You can think of a My Block as a small program within a large program. It is called a My Block because it is a block that you create.

At the beginning, the robot will move forward until the Wait block is triggered by a change in state of the Touch Sensor. We will then program the robot to move back for one rotation of the wheels and display the following message onto the brick screen: **Press left or right**. The next Wait block will wait for the user to press one of the brick buttons on the EV3 brick. This will be followed by a case structure or Switch Flow block.

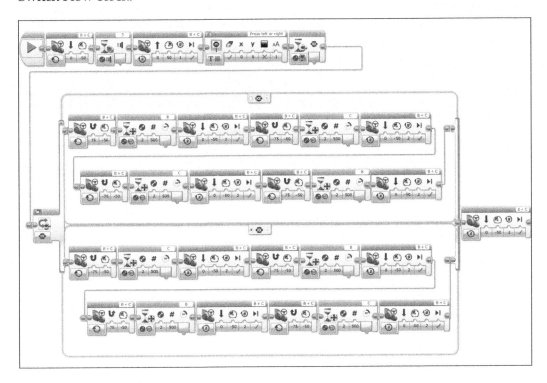

The Switch Flow block has two cases, one if the left brick button is depressed and the other if the right brick button is depressed. Note that the default case of the case structure is actually the second case. So the right button does not actually have to be pushed. If any button other than the left button is pushed, the second case will be chosen. The user will determine if they want the robot to avoid the obstacle by taking a detour around the left side or around the right side of the obstacle. Each case contains 11 blocks. The following command blocks inside the case, we can see the robot will turn until the Motor Rotation Wait block tells it to stop. The robot will then move forward, turn, and repeat. The sequence is quite long. You should also note that we alternate between using the rotation sensor on port B and port C. This is because, while turning, one of the wheels travels farther than the other. We want to use the outside wheel to keep track of the quantity of our motion. Later in the chapter, we will explore a trick to get around this.

At this point, we can download and execute the code and the robot should be able to steer around a small rigid object.

We can now simplify the code using a My Block or subroutine. Select all of the blocks inside one branch of the case structure. To select several blocks, you should click and drag a box around the blocks you want to select. You will know the blocks have been selected because they will be highlighted with a light blue perimeter. Then, from the pull down menus, navigate to **Tools | My Block Builder**, as you can see in the following screenshot:

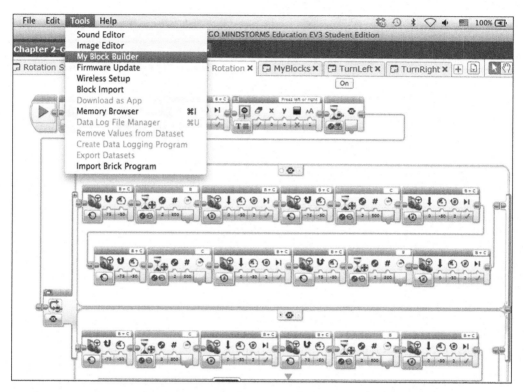

The **My Block Builder** screen will pop up and ask you to name the My Block, which is akin to naming a subroutine. You can also write a description and select an icon. You can also design an icon. We will name this My Block LeftTurn. I have chosen a rotation sensor as the visual icon, as shown in the following screenshot:

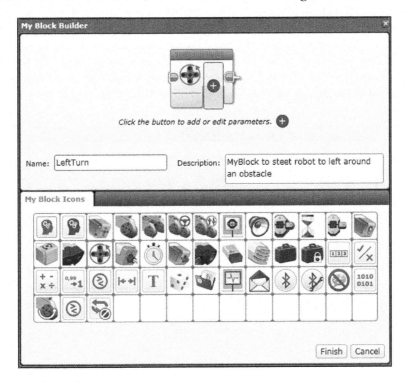

You might also notice that the My Block can be modified to accept parameters. Do not press the **Finish** button yet. It is not possible to alter the parameter setup of My Block once you have created it. In our program, input parameters will be useful, so we can make quick changes to the maximum amount of rotations the Motor Rotation sensor Wait block has to wait for without needing to use a variable. You can see in the following screenshot that I have chosen a slider to alter this parameter and set the limits to 0 and 1000 degrees of rotation for the sensor. Note that My Block can also be created in such a way that it accepts wires for the input and output parameters. Some advance planning for the My Block creation is needed because, as mentioned earlier, it is not possible to alter the parameter setup of My Block once you have created it.

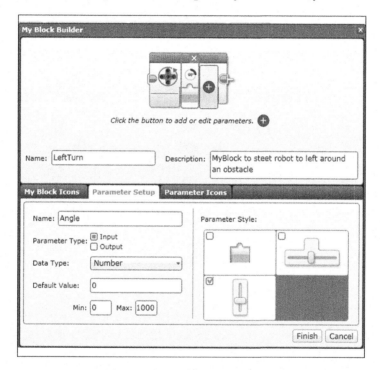

In the preceding screenshot, you can see that I have chosen a rotation icon for the input parameter, which I call Angle. You can choose **Parameter Icons** by clicking on the third tab of the My Block Builder screen.

You should do the same for the other branch of the case structure (or switch), but instead, name that My Block TurnRight. At this point, we can clean up the code by deleting a lot of the empty space that has been created inside the Switch block, as you can see in the following screenshot:

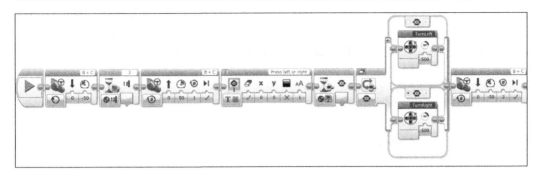

After you have defined a My Block, you can find it in the Programming Palette under the commands in the light blue programming blocks tab. Before we run this program, we need to make some small changes inside My Block. If you double-click on My Block, you can see what is under the hood. If you are using input and output parameters, you will need to connect the wires from those parameters to the blocks inside My Block. In this base, I have drawn wires from the input parameter to all of the Wait Motor Rotation sensor blocks:

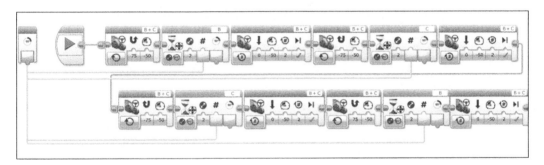

Here, I have done the same thing for the My Block TurnRight:

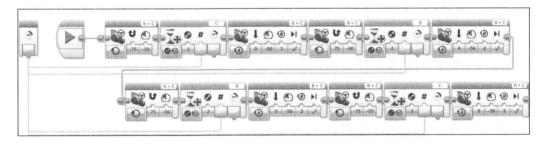

We can now download and execute this simplified code. After this Motor Rotation sensor-driven solution, you can now try to make My Blocks for the Gyro version of this program, which you will find in the following screenshot:

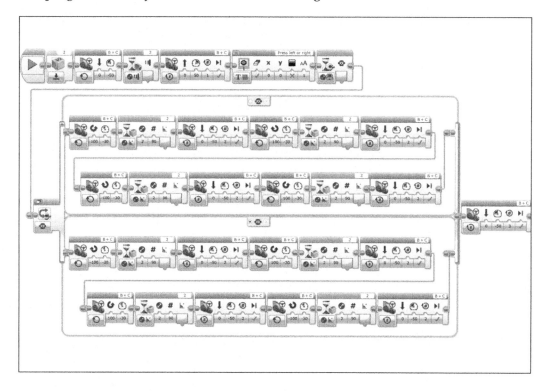

Arrays

We just saw how to simplify the program to avoid an obstacle using a My Block (subroutine). Now, we will instead optimize the program using an array, whereas in the LEGO EV3 software, a variable can have one value, an array can have several elements, each with its own value. To learn how an array in EV3 works, you will first need to write a program to display a series of numbers on the EV3 brick screen.

First, clear the display screen. Then define a variable called steering. By clicking on the mode selector of the Variable block, we can choose to write to an array instead of writing to a numeric variable. The LEGO EV3 software contains numeric and logic (or Boolean) arrays. It does not currently have arrays for strings (or lists).

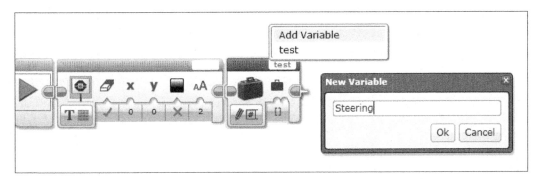

We will write the series of numbers [100, -100, -100, 100] into the array. You can enter elements by clicking on the input value of the array variable block. This will be useful later when we use this same array variable block in the obstacle code.

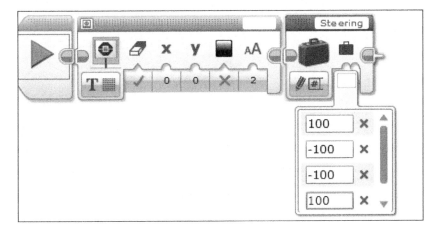

We will now create a loop called Display Steering that will repeat four times. The first block in our loop will read array variable block. It will then send the information from the variable via a wire steering into an array operation block. The plugs for an array wire have two semicircles. Notice that the wire for an array is much thicker than the wires for numeric data. We will also run a wire from the loop index into the array operation. This will allow us to read a different element in the array every iteration of the loop. This element will be sent as text to the display screen via a wire. Remember to uncheck the clear screen parameter on the Display block so that it will not erase each time it runs. Again, the y coordinate location on the display screen is increased by a multiple of the loop index.

When you run this program, you should see the elements of the array displayed in a column on the brick screen every 2 seconds.

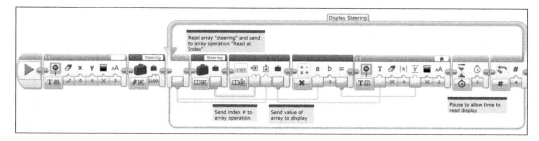

Now we are going to use an array to modify the obstacle code we wrote earlier. Let's first examine the version of our program using the Gyro Sensor. You will need to add the write array variable block in the beginning of the program before the case structure.

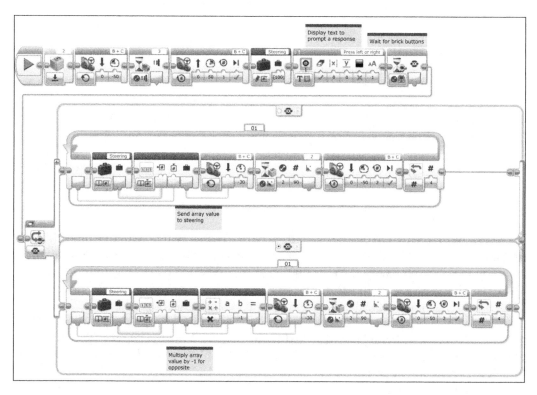

Replace the code you previously wrote in the left button case structure with the following blocks:

1. First, place a loop that will run for 4 counts into the case structure.

2. Next, send the output from a read array variable block to an array operation block.

3. Run a wire from the loop index to the array operation block.

4. Then run a wire from the array operation block output to the move steering block direction input.

The array is telling the robot in which direction to turn. Remember, the array contains the elements [100, -100, -100, 100]. If the program chooses the first or last elements, then the steering value is to the left. If the program chooses the second or third elements, then the steering value is to the right. During each loop, the element that is chosen is determined by the loop index. The robot will turn until the Wait Gyro block reaches 90 degrees. The robot will then move forward for two rotations of the wheel and the loop will repeat.

The other side of the case structure, resulting when the right (or any other) button is pushed, has a similar code. We can modify the direction of the robot by adding a Math block, which will send the negative of the value of the array elements to the Move Steering block.

Now, let's examine a version of the array code using the rotation sensor and dead reckoning. The code is almost identical to the Gyro array code. With the My Block code, we paid careful attention to which wheel we monitored for the number of rotations. However, we also used a gentle turning (75 percent) so that the wheels were not turning at the same rate. In this array code, the turning rates of the wheels are at 100 percent. In a full speed turn, the wheels will rotate exactly opposite of each other. This means that for every forward rotation of the motor connected to port B, the motor connected to port C rotates once backwards.

Thus, we are not concerned about which motor rotation sensor we are monitoring. This is a very useful trick in dead reckoning.

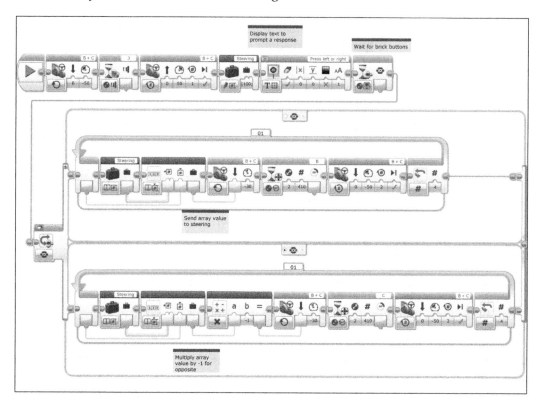

Summary

In this chapter, we explored various programming techniques such as My Blocks, Switches, and Loops. We used combinations of switches and loops to cause our robot to drive in a square and avoid an obstacle. We used two-level and three-level controllers to help us navigate and make precise turns. You learned how to navigate using both dead reckoning and the Gyro Sensor. You learned how to simplify your programs using My Blocks and Arrays.

In the next chapter, we will develop a proportional controller that determines the position using either the Ultrasonic or the Infrared Sensor. We will also develop a proportional line following robot using the Color Sensor.

8
Advanced Programming and Control

In this chapter, we will explore advanced controlling algorithms to use for sensor-based navigation and tracking. We will cover:

- Proportional distance control with the Ultrasonic Sensor
- Proportional distance control with the Infrared (IR) Sensor
- Line following with the Color Sensor
- Two-level control with the Color Sensor
- Proportional control with the Color Sensor
- Proportional integral derivative control
- Precise turning and course correction with the Gyro Sensor
- Beacon tracking with the IR sensor
- Triangulation with two IR beacons

Distance controller

In this section, we will program the robot to gradually come to a stop using a proportional algorithm. In *Chapter 4, Sensors and Control*, we wrote a program where the robot would stop a set distance from a barrier using feedback from the distance sensors. These programs used a discrete reading where the robot would run at full speed until the sensor feedback triggered the robot to abruptly stop. In a proportional algorithm, the robot will gradually slow down as it approaches the desired stopping point.

Before we begin, we need to attach a distance sensor to our robot. If you have the Home Edition, you will be using the IR sensor, whereas if you have the Educational Edition, you will use the Ultrasonic Sensor. Because these sensors use reflected beams (infrared light or sound), they need to be placed unobstructed by the other parts of the robot. You could either place the sensor high above the robot or well out in front of many parts of the robot.

The design I have shown in the following screenshot allows you to place the sensor in front of the robot. If you are using the Ultrasonic Sensor for FIRST Lego League (a competition that uses a lot of sensor-based navigation) and trying to measure the distance to the border, you will find it is a good idea to place the sensor as low as possible. This is because the perimeter of the playing fields for FIRST LEGO League are made from 3- or 4-inch- high pieces of lumber.

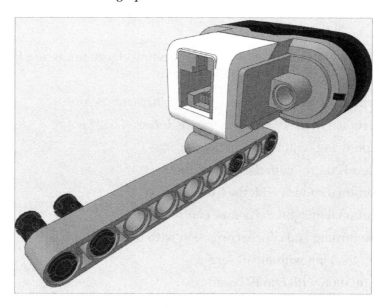

Infrared versus Ultrasonic

We are going to start out with a simple program and will gradually add complexity to it. If you are using the Ultrasonic Sensor, it should be plugged into port 4, and this program is on the top line. If you are using the IR sensor, it should be plugged into port 1 and this program is at the bottom line. In this program, the robot moves forward until the Wait block tells it to stop 25 units from a wall or other barrier. You will find that the Ultrasonic Sensor can be set to stop in units of inches or centimeters. The Ultrasonic Sensor emits high-frequency sound waves (above the range of human hearing) and measures the time delay between the emission of the sound waves and when the reflection off an object is measured by the sensor.

In everyday conditions, we can assume that the speed of sound is constant, and thus the Ultrasonic Sensor can give precise distance measurements to the nearest centimeter. As mentioned in *Chapter 4*, *Sensors and Control*, using presence we could use the Ultrasonic Sensor to detect other robots or a loud sound. In other programming languages, you could even use the Ultrasonic Sensor to transmit data between two robots. The IR sensor emits infrared light and has an IR-sensitive camera that measures the reflected light. The sensor reading does not give exact distance units because the strength of the signal depends on environmental factors such as the reflectivity of the surface. What the IR sensor loses in precision in proximity measurements, it makes up for in the fact that you can use it to track on the IR beacon, which is a source of infrared light. In other programming languages, you could actually use the IR sensor to track on sources of infrared light other than the beacon (such as humans or animals).

In the following screenshot, we have a simple program that will tell the robot to stop a given distance from a barrier using a Wait for the sensor block. The program on the top of the screenshot uses the Ultrasonic Sensor, and the program on the bottom of the screenshot uses the IR sensor. You should only use the program for the sensor you are using. If you are downloading and executing the program from the Packt Publishing website, you should delete the program that you do not need.

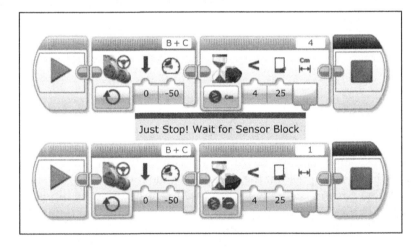

When you execute the program in the preceding screenshot, you will find that the robot only begins to stop at 25 units from the wall, but cannot stop immediately. To do this, the robot will need to slow down before it gets to the stopping point.

Proportional algorithm

In the next set of program, we create a loop called Slow Down. Inside this loop, readings from the Ultrasonic or Infrared proximity sensor block are sent to a Math block (to take the negative of the position values so that the robot moves forward) and then sent to the power input of a Move Steering block. We can have the loop end when it reaches our desired stopping distance as shown in the following screenshot:

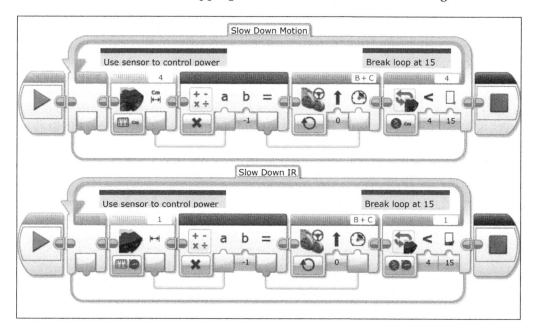

Instead of using the exact values of the output of the sensor block, we can use the difference between the actual position and the desired position to control the Move Steering block, as shown in the following screenshot. This difference is called the error. We call the desired position the setpoint. In the following screenshot, the setpoint is **20**. The power is actually *proportional* to the error or the difference between the positions. When you execute this code, you will also find that if the robot is too close to the wall, it will run in reverse and back up from the wall.

We are using an Advanced Math block in the following screenshot. You can see that we are writing a simple equation, - (a-b), into the block text field of the Advanced Math block:

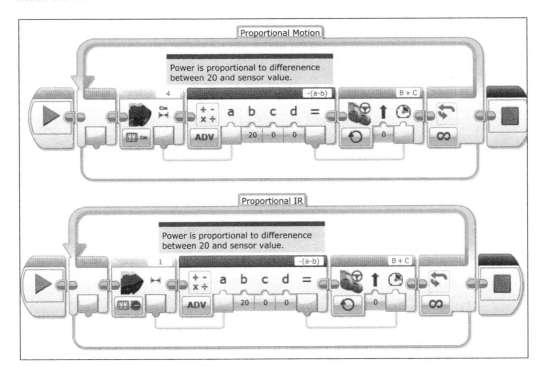

You may have also noticed that the robot moves very slowly as it approaches the stopping point. You can change this program by adding gain to the algorithm. If you multiply the difference by a larger factor, it will approach the stopping point quicker. When you execute this program, you will find that if you increase the gain too much, it will overshoot the stopping point and reverse direction. We can adjust these values using the Advanced Math block. We can type in any simple math function we need, as shown in the following screenshot. In this block, the value of *a* is the measured position, *b* is the setpoint position, and *c* is the gain.

The equation can be seen in the following screenshot inside the block text field of the Advanced Math block:

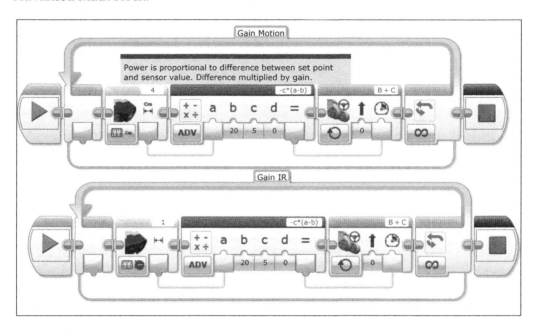

We can also define the desired gain and setpoint position using variables. We can create two Variable blocks called Gain and Set Point. We can write the value 3 to the Gain variable block and 20 to the Set Point variable block. Inside our loop, we can then read these variables and take the output of the Read Variable block and draw data wires into the Advanced Math block.

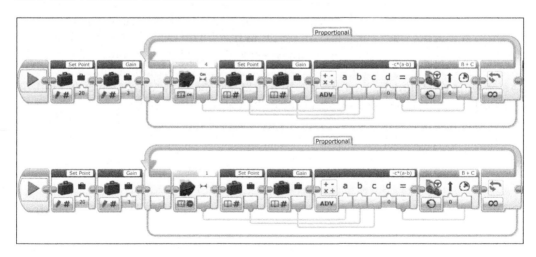

The basic idea of the proportional algorithm is that the degree of correction needed is proportional to the error. So when our measured value is far from our goal, a large correction is applied. When our measured value is near our goal, only a small correction is applied. The algorithm also allows overcorrections. If the robot moves past the setpoint distance, it will back up. Depending on what you are trying to do, you will need to play around with various values for the gain variable. If the gain is too large, you will overshoot your goal and oscillate around it. If your gain is too small, you will never reach your goal. The response time of the microprocessor also affects the efficiency of the algorithm. You can experiment by inserting a Wait block into the loop and see how this affects the behavior of the robot.

If we are merely using the distance sensor to approach a stationary object, then the proportional algorithm will suffice. However, if you were trying to maintain a given distance from a moving object (such as another robot), you might need a more complicated algorithm such as a **Proportional Integral Derivative (PID)** controller. Next we will build a line follower using the Color Sensor, which will use a PID controller.

Line following using the Color Sensor

When we are using the Color Sensor in Reflected Light Intensity mode, the sensor emits light and the robot measures the intensity of the reflected light. The brightness of the red LED in the sensor is a constant, but the intensity of the reflection will depend on the reflectivity of the surface, the angle of the sensor relative to the surface, and the distance of the sensor from the surface. If you shine the sensor at a surface, you will notice that a circle of light is generated. As you change the height of the sensor, the diameter of this circle will change because the light emitted from the LED diverges in a cone. As you increase the height, the size of the circle gets larger and the reflected intensity gets smaller. You might think you want the sensor to be as close as possible to the surface. Because there is a finite distance between the LED and the photo diode (which collects the light) of about 5.5 mm, it puts a constraint on the minimum diameter of your circle of light. Ideally, you want the circle of light to have a diameter of about 11 mm, which means placing the sensor about half of a centimeter above the tracking surface.

Because the height of the EV3 brick is different for each of the four robots I presented in *Chapter 3, Drive Train and Chassis*, I will give you a design for attaching the Color Sensor at the proper height for each of those robots.

For the caster-bot, you will need the sensor, an axle, two bushings, two long pins, a 5-mod beam, and two axle-pin connectors, as you can see in the following screenshot:

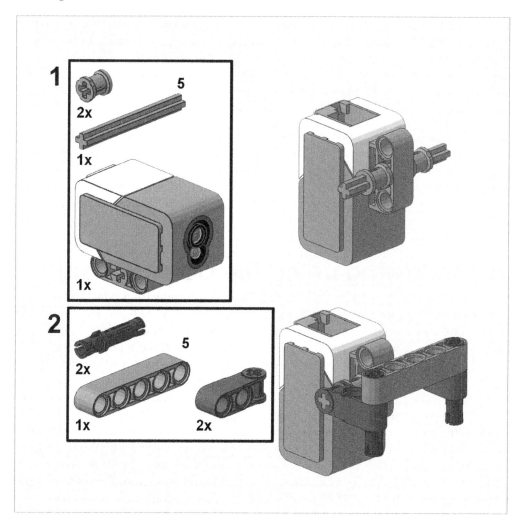

You can assemble the sensor attachment in two steps. The sensor attachment settles into the holes in the caster attachment itself as you can see in the following screenshot. This placement is ideal as it allows the caster to do the steering while you do your line tracking.

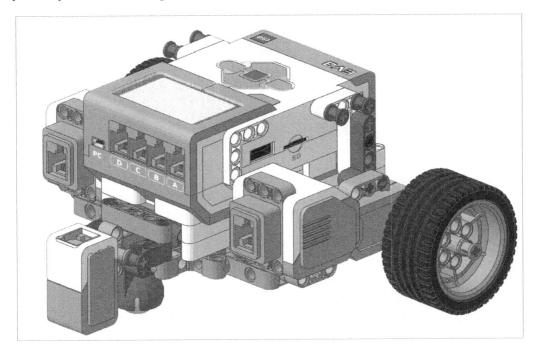

You can build the Color Sensor attachment in four steps. The Color Sensor attachment for the skid-bot will be the most complicated of our designs because we want the sensor to be in front of the robot and the skid is quite long.

Again, we will need the pins, axles, bushings, and axle-pin connectors seen in the following screenshot:

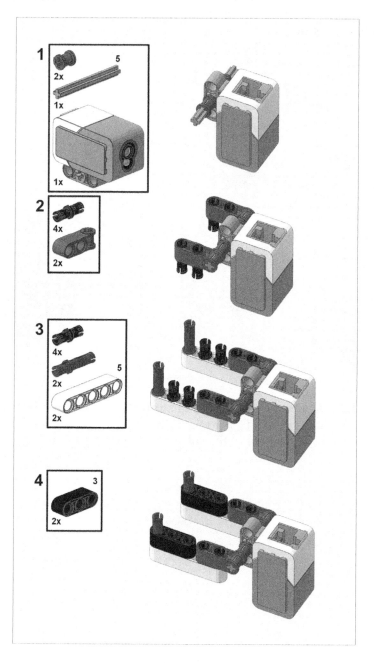

The Color Sensor attachment will connect directly to the EV3 brick. As you can see in the following screenshot, the attachment will be inserted from below the brick:

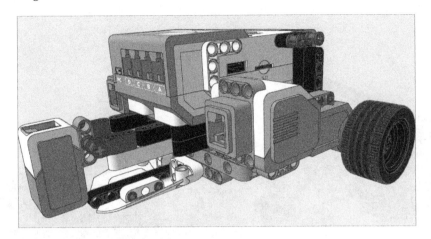

Next I will describe the attachment for the tread-bot from the Educational kit. Because the tread-bot is slightly higher off the ground, we need to use some pieces such as the thin 1 x 4 mod lift arm that is a half mod in height. This extra millimeter in height can make a huge difference in the signal strength. The pins have trouble gripping the thin lift arm, so I like to use the pins with stop bushings to prevent the lift arm from falling off.

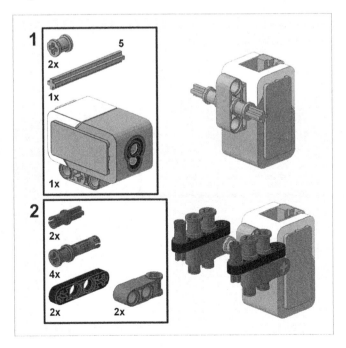

The Light Sensor attachment is once again inserted into the underside of the EV3 brick as you can see in the following screenshot:

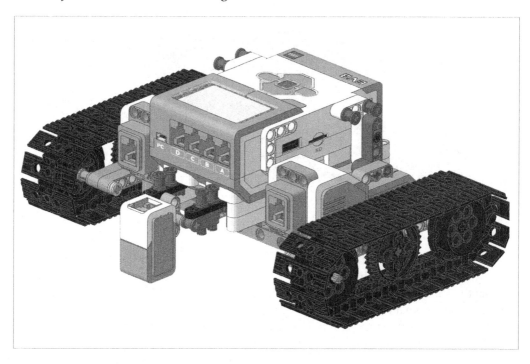

The simplest of our Light Sensor attachments will be the tread-bot for the Home Edition, and you can build this in one step.

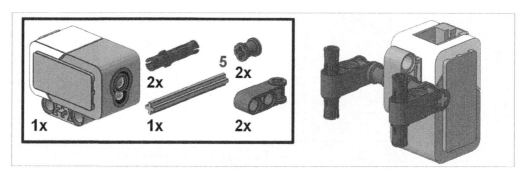

Similarly, it attaches to the underside of the EV3 brick.

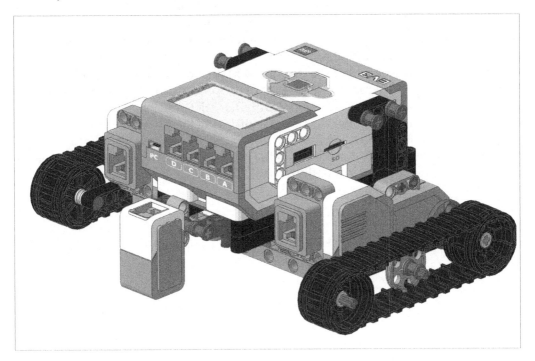

Setpoint for line tracking

We first need to determine the desired setpoint of the Light Sensor reading for the robot to track on. When using only one sensor, we don't want to track the middle of the line because small changes in position will not be sensed. If we track along the edge of a line, then a small change in position will substantially affect the size of the correction error in our algorithm. In this case, 50 percent of the circle of red light will have a high reflectivity and 50 percent will have a low reflectivity. Small deviations from the edge will result in huge changes in the measured intensity. Placing the middle of the circle of light exactly on the edge can be a challenge. Since we are trying to obtain a numerical value, it is easier to separately measure the high reflection intensity and low reflection intensity and find the average of those two values.

You will find that you will frequently determine a new setpoint value based on your environmental conditions. In addition to the actual reflectivity of the surface material, the ambient room light (including shadows) can also affect your setpoint value. For all of our light tracking robots, you should have the Color Sensor plugged into port 3 on your EV3 brick.

In the following screenshot, you can see a program I have written that will allow you to record the setpoint and save this to a file in the memory on the EV3 brick. This is a calibration program, and other programs will read the calibration value file later. This type of program can be very useful at robot competitions, where you are allowed a limited amount of time to take a Color Sensor calibration reading on the playing fields. The output of the Advanced Math block is connected by a wire to the Write File block. Before we write to the file, we initialize the file by deleting any information that may be there before with the Delete File block. After we have written the information, we need to close the file using the Close File block. This program takes a Light Sensor reading and saves it to the file light. By saving the setpoint to a file, it saves us the need to either alter the program with the computer or continuously enter a setpoint with the brick buttons.

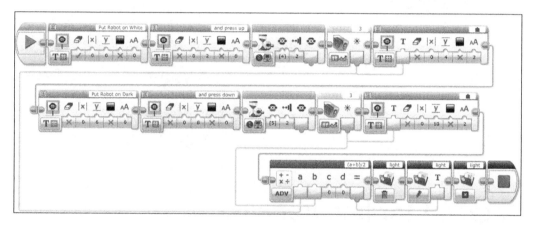

Two-level or bang-bang controller

When we looked at the simplest of distance controllers, we simply used a Wait block to tell the robot to stop. However, as we are tracking a line, our conditions relative to the line are constantly changing as the line may move straight or curve. The simplest controller is called a two-level or bang-bang controller. If the sensor measures a reading greater than the setpoint, the robot will curve to the left. If the sensor measures a reading less than the setpoint, the robot will drive to the right.

When you execute the program in the following screenshot, you will notice that the robot will follow a zigzag type of motion along the line:

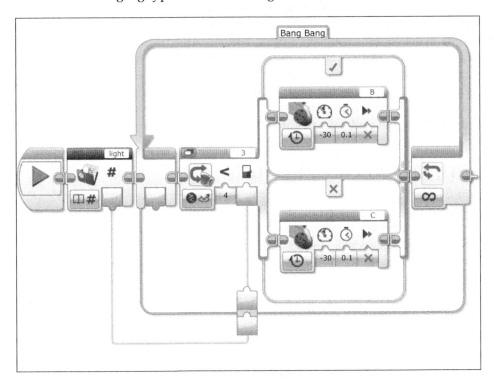

In the program itself, you may notice that we read the value of the setpoint from the Read File block. You can actually take data from an external source into the loop, and this is shown with the splice in the wire at the edge of the loop. Alternatively, you could store the information from the File block into a variable. Then the Variable block could be placed inside of the loop. This saves the need to read from a file each time the loop runs.

Inside the loop, you can see that we have a case structure. The case structure is controlled by the reflected light intensity of the Color Sensor. If the reflected light intensity is greater than the setpoint, then the motor plugged into port C drives forward. If the reflected light intensity is less than the setpoint, then the motor plugged into port B drives forward.

Using additional switch blocks, you could create a three-level controller where the robot drives forward if it is very close to following the edge of the line. Even with this improvement, however, the bang-bang controller lacks smoothness and efficiency.

Proportional line follower

The proportional algorithm will make a correction to the motor speeds, which is proportional to the magnitude of the error between the setpoint and the sensor value. Each wheel has a given base speed, which we correct by either adding or subtracting a factor proportional to the error. If the right wheel is faster, the robot turns to the left. If the left wheel is faster, the robot will turn to the right. A critical number for efficient line tracking is the proportional gain constant. If the gain is too large, the robot will overcompensate for errors and wiggle back and forth. If the gain is too small, the robot will have trouble following tighter curves.

Entering gain and speed

You could enter the gain and speed directly by reprogramming the robot. However, to save ourselves time in adjusting the setpoint, gain, and speed of the robot, let's first write two more programs to enter the speed and gain factors. The program in the following screenshot will allow you to use the brick buttons to adjust the gain in your program and store that information in a File block called Gain.

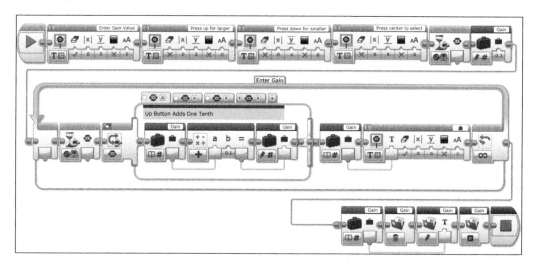

The preceding screenshot has the Switch block in the tabbed view. The following screenshot will show the Switch block in its expanded view:

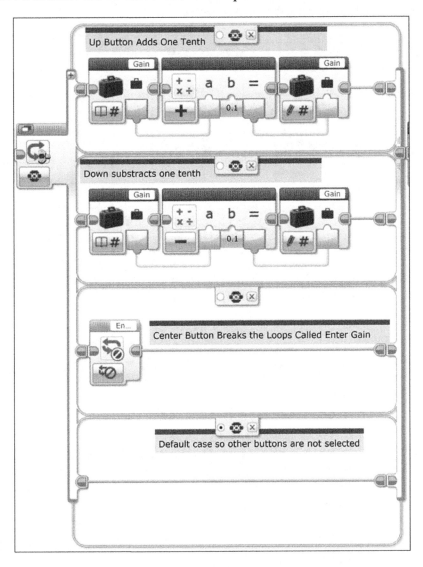

Similarly, we have another program to enter a speed for our robot. I find that when I first build a robot and experiment with a line, I like to have the robot start out slowly and then gradually increase values for the speed.

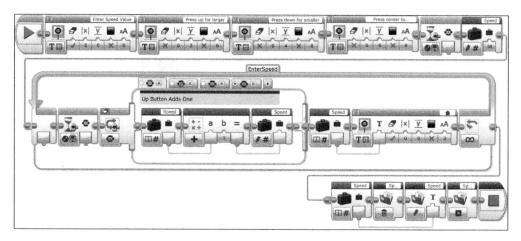

The preceding screenshot has the Switch block in the tabbed view. The following screenshot will show the Switch block in its expanded view:

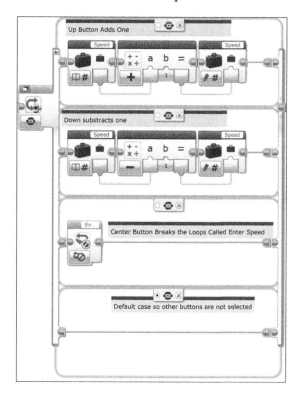

Once we have our values for the gain, the setpoint, and the speed of our robot, the proportional algorithm is rather straightforward. The program finds the difference between the setpoint and the sensor. This error is adjusted by multiplying it with the proportional gain constant, which is probably between 0 and 1. I suggest starting out with a value of around 0.7. The result or correction is added to the base speed of one motor and subtracted from the base speed of the other motor. It will take some trial and error to determine the best speed and proportionality gain constants to make your robot follow a line.

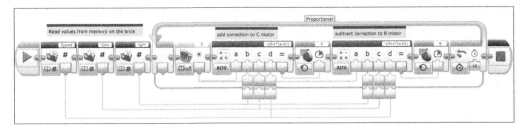

If you wanted to bypass using the File access blocks in the preceding program, you could replace them with variable blocks and then change the program using your computer as you experiment.

PID controller

One of the limitations of the proportional controller is that a value for the gain in your program might be ideal for only one type of curve. For instance, the parameters that work well for tracking a straight line might not work as well on sharp curves. In some instances, the correction might not be strong enough, and in others, your robot might overcorrect. The PID controller attempts to compensate for these environmental variations.

We have already discussed the ideas behind the proportional controller. The strength of the correction is proportional to the error of how far our sensor reading is from the setpoint. If we are consistently having to include a large and consistent correction (say we are always a bit too far off the edge of the line), then we must have needed a stronger gain. The way to account for this on the fly is to have the robot remember that it has been consistently off the line (or too far above/below the setpoint) for a period of time and increase the correction. This is the integral controller portion of the PID controller. In simplified mathematical terms, an integral means to add up the values of a function or parameter over a given range. The integral controller adds up the recent values of the errors and adds an additional correction to that of the proportional controller.

We also include a dampening term, so we do not remember too far back in time and the influence of previous errors gets smaller after several iterations of the loop. In the case of two robots (or cars) trying to maintain a given distance of separation, the integral controller would tell the second robot if it has room to speed up, or if it has been too close for too long and it needs to slow down even more.

However, if our corrections and our gain are too strong, we will approach the setpoint too quickly and overshoot our goal. The derivative controller attempts to prevent wobbling if things are happening too fast. In mathematical terms, the derivative refers to the rate of change of a parameter, or how quickly a value is changing, so if the error is decreasing (or increasing) too quickly, then the derivative controller will step up and dampen the corrections. The derivative controller using our distance sensors might prevent us from having a collision if the proportional and integral terms are not slowing us down quickly enough.

In the following screenshot, I present a basic PID controller using the Color Sensor. You can find more information on LEGO PID controllers on the blogs of Jim Sluka (`http://www.inpharmix.com/jps/PID_Controller_For_Lego_Mindstorms_Robots.html`) or Miguel Lardin (`http://thetechnicgear.com/2014/03/howto-create-line-following-robot-using-mindstorms/`). Their controllers might appear simpler as I have defined all six of my parameters using variable blocks in the first row of the program. I try not to bury the variables inside of the math functions. Although this makes the program longer and seemingly more complicated, this simplifies the process of changing the values of these parameters. These parameters include Speed, Gain, Set Point, K-Deriv, Dampen, and K-Integral. We have mentioned Speed, Gain and Set Point before. The derivative constant, or K-Deriv, is a multiplier to increase the strength of the derivative controller in our program. The integral constant, or K-Integral, is a multiplier to increase the strength of the integral controller in our program. Because our integral controller does not remember too far back, we also include the Dampen constant, which needs to be a value between 0 and 1.

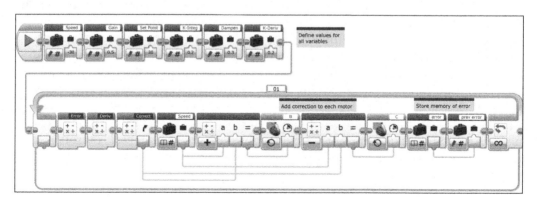

In the second row of the program, I used several My Blocks to simplify the program. The error My Block will calculate the error and the integral terms. You can see inside of the error My Block in the following screenshot. We first calculate the value of the error Variable block, which is the difference between the sensor reading and the setpoint. Next we calculate the integral. The new value of the integral is the sum of the error and the dampened value of the integral. Each iteration of the loop creates a new integral value based on the old integral value and the new updated error. The dampen constant has a compounding affect, so after a few iterations, the memory of the old errors is trivial.

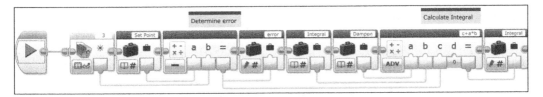

In the Deriv My Block, which we can see in the following screenshot, we calculate the value of the Derivative Variable block. The derivative is the difference of the current error and the error from the previous iteration, multiplied by the derivative constant, K-Deriv. If this difference between the errors is zero, then there is no derivative correction.

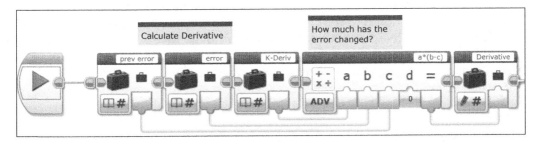

In the Correct My Block, which is in the following screenshot, we add together the corrections due to these three controlling algorithms. We first add the derivative and integral corrections together. Then we add in the proportional correction. Because the Advanced Math blocks only allow four terms, we had to break this up into a couple of steps.

If you look on the right-hand side of the following screenshot, you will see that the output from the second Math Block is connected by a wire to an output plug. This allows the value of the summed correction to leave the Correct My Block as we saw in the main program.

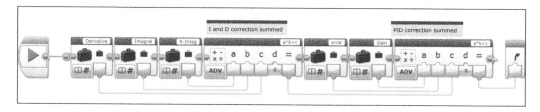

Returning to the main program, we use this summed correction to either increase or decrease the motor speed of the driving wheels. We can see in the preceding screenshot of the main program that a wire from the output plug of the Correct My Block goes into the Math blocks. We finish the loop by storing the value of the error variable block into the previous error variable block.

Once you have the program, the hardest part is determining good values for your robot to follow its track. Similar to the simple proportional controller, you will find that you may need different values for different tracks. A full explanation of the mathematics behind tuning the constants in a PID controller is beyond the scope of this text, but there are dozens of in-depth blogs and wiki pages on the subject. The most common suggestion is to start with 0 values for the integral and derivative controllers. You then increase your gain variable until the robots begin to oscillate. Decrease your gain by about half and slowly add in the integral controller constant. Once you have done this, you can tweak things as needed with the derivative controller constant.

Gyro Sensor

In *Chapter 4, Sensors and Control,* when we introduced the Gyro Sensor, we wrote a program that stopped the rotation of the robot when the Gyro Sensor reached a certain value. As we noticed, the robot always overshot this value. In *Chapter 7, Advanced Programming,* we tried to compensate for the overshooting with a two-level controller. Here we show a program where the measurement from the Gyro Sensor goes into a proportional controller.

You will find that this method is significantly more precise and useful in making exact turns.

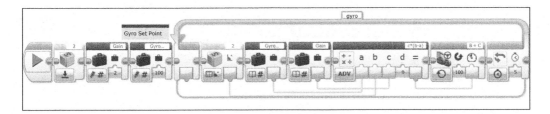

The preceding program asks the robot to rotate through a given angle and slow to a stop. If we used a smaller gain constant, we could avoid using a loop. However, this can take more time and runs the risk of never reaching your setpoint. This is similar to approaching a set distance from a wall using the motion or proximity sensors. Again, we start out by resetting the Gyro.

A more interesting use of the Gyro Sensor will be to drive in a straight line under constantly changing conditions. This algorithm is akin to line tracking along a curving line. Suppose you are attempting to drive straight while pushing an object (such as a LEGO car or truck with wheels). There will be a lot of friction, which will easily push your robot off course. The following program will allow the robot to constantly correct itself, so it maintains a course direction given by the Gyro.

We begin the program by defining values for our speed, gain, and set point variable blocks. Inside of the loop, the second line of our program calculates a proportional correction to how far off the robot is from the setpoint angle. We then add this correction to one wheel and subtract from the other wheel. Notice that to reduce the number of blocks in this case, I used a Move Tank block with each correction connected to a different wheel. In a Move Tank block, the power level for each wheel has its own input plug.

In a Move Steering block, there is one input plug for power and one input plug for direction.

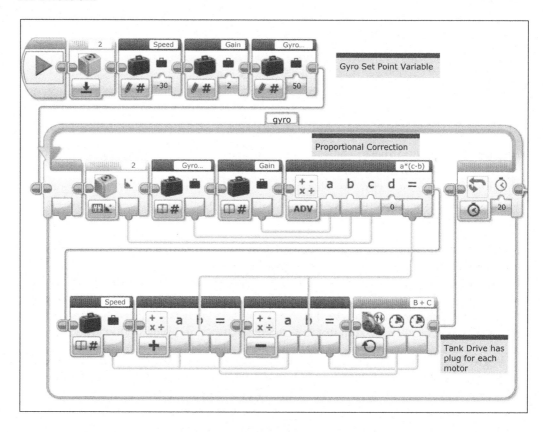

If the robot is not pushing a load, you will find it drives straight easily. As it drives, give it a push and you will find it will correct its course.

IR sensor navigation and beacon tracking

One of the simplest uses of the IR sensor and the IR beacon is to have the robot seek out the beacon. The program to have the robot seek the beacon is simple and again uses a proportional controller. The sensor block values of heading for the beacon range from -25 to 25. In the following program, my correction is going into the steering plug of a Move Steering block. Since the steering input values of the Move Steering block range from -100 to 100, you want to have a gain of 4 in the program. Make sure your beacon is set to the same channel as your sensor block, which in this case is channel 1.

If your robot turns in the wrong direction, you can either swap which cable the motors are connected to or change the gain constant to -4.

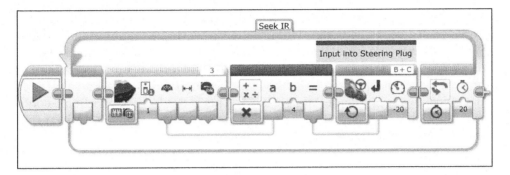

Navigating a field with the IR sensor and the beacon may not be as obvious as using the Ultrasonic motion sensor and the Gyro Sensor. However, if you read about approach paths used in aviation using non-directional beacons, a Gyro, and distance measuring devices, you will find that you can come up with incredibly sophisticated navigation programs.

Tracking a circle

Using the beacon and the IR sensor, you can program your robot to drive in a circle while maintaining a constant radius relative to the beacon. To do this, the IR sensor should be mounted on the robot pointed to the side as shown in the following screenshot. The robot should be set up to drive a circumference of a circle.

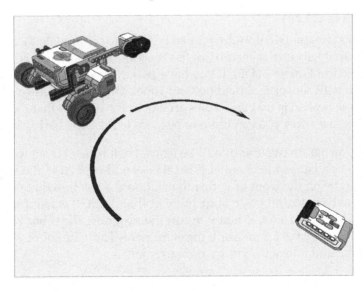

Remember, the IR beacon has a limited cone of emission, so you will need to start the robot within about a 45 degree cone of the front of the beacon. This program will work better for larger distances (more than a meter). Your gain constant values will vary depending on the type of robot you use. If you were to set the beacon standing on its end, you can actually track a wider circle. However, the radius will be smaller when the robot travels around the back of the beacon since there is opaque plastic blocking some of the signal. To do this, you should use a smaller radius of about half a meter. The program starts out by sending the proximity to the beacon value of the IR sensor block to the Set Point Variable block. This is used as a proportional control for the robot within the Loop. Pilots call this type of navigation flying a **Distance Measuring Equipment (DME)** arc.

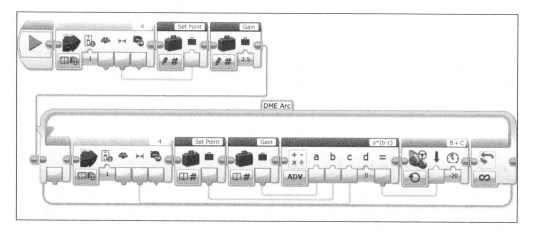

Triangulation

In aviation, pilots can use two non-directional beacons to triangulate their position. The instrument that tells us the heading of the beacons on an airplane is called the **Automatic Direction Finder (ADF)**. If you have two IR beacons, you can do a similar thing with just one IR sensor mounted on your robot. One disadvantage of the heading indicator from the beacon is that the values are not in the degrees that the Gyro Sensor uses. Still, with some effort you can use two beacons to do some basic triangulation.

In the following program, we use two IR beacons. Each beacon is set to a different channel. Set the first beacon to channel 1. Set the second beacon to channel 2. The IR sensor should be on the front of your robot. Choose a location that you want the robot to navigate back to and place your robot at that point. It is helpful to angle the beacons towards the robot. When you run the program, the robot will first turn towards beacon 1 and take a proximity measurement. Then the robot will turn towards beacon 2 and take a proximity measurement.

The value of the proximity measurement can change with the heading of the robot, so you do need to have the robot pointed straight towards the beacon for reproducible results. After you have done this, the robot can be moved to another location. After a brick button is pushed, the robot will navigate back to its original position.

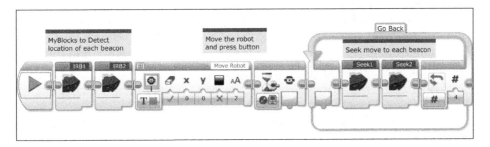

Since this is a complex program, we will use My Blocks to make it easier to follow. In the preceding screenshot, you can see the first two My Blocks, **IRB1** and **IRB2**, which will record the proximity measurements of the two beacons. The robot then waits for a brick button to signal that it has been repositioned. We then enter a loop where My Block **Seek1** commands the robot to turn towards beacon 1, and then move toward it. Although we do not know the exact location of the robot, we know it is on a circular arc near beacon 1. Next, in My Block **Seek2**, the robot turns towards beacon 2 and then moves towards beacon 2. This loop repeats itself four times, which should be enough to reach the original location.

Let's now examine the program inside each of the My Blocks that will record the proximity measurements of the beacons.

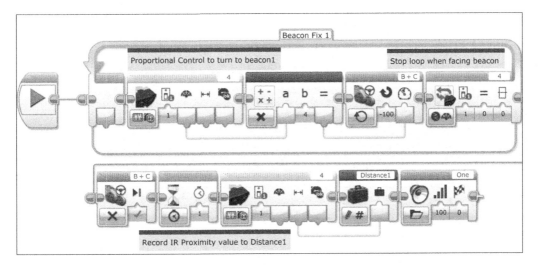

In the preceding screenshot, we can see the program inside of My Block IRB1. The robot begins by turning towards the infrared beacon, which is set for channel 1. The robot only turns and does not move towards the beacon. The loop stops when the robot is facing the beacon. The robot will then pause (to make sure there is no motion) and store the proximity value from the Infrared Sensor to the Variable block **Distance1**. The robot will announce with the speaker that it has detected the first beacon. In the following screenshot, we can see a similar program inside of My Block IRB2. The main difference is that the sensor block is set to channel 2, and the value is stored to the variable **Distance2**.

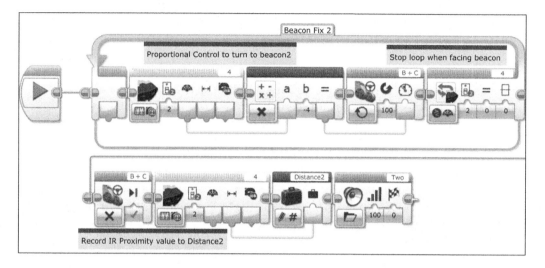

We will now examine the program inside each seek My Block that will navigate the robot back to the original position.

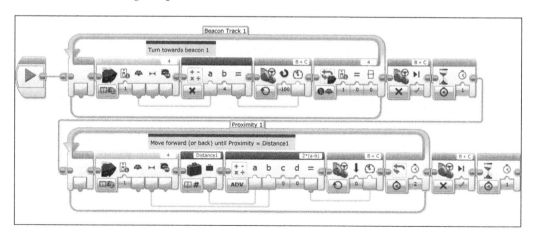

As we can see in the preceding screenshot, our **Seek1** My Block begins with a loop, which is similar to the previous My Blocks. The robot starts out by turning towards the beacon. When it is facing the beacon, the robot pauses to allow it to come to a complete stop. The robot will then move forwards (or backwards) proportionally to the error between the proximity value of the Infrared Sensor and the distance Variable block. In the following screenshot, you can see the **Seek2** My Block. The only difference is the channel for the sensor block and the Variable block.

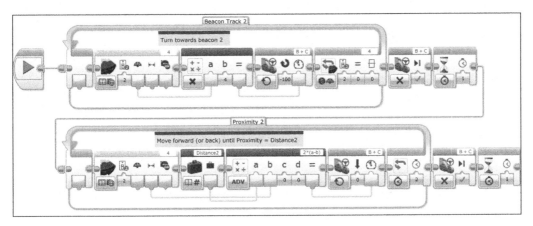

If you were to combine the information of the Gyro Sensor and the Infrared sensor, you would have an even more powerful tool to navigate a course. The Gyro Sensor would allow you to know along which radial your robot is positioned relative to the beacon.

Summary

In this chapter, we explored advanced methods of navigations. We used both the Ultrasonic Sensor and the Infrared sensor to measure distance with a proportional algorithm. We used the Color Sensor with a two-level, proportional, and PID algorithm. We used the Gyro Sensor for a proportional algorithm and course corrections. Finally, we used the IR sensor with the IR beacon to navigate with several advanced techniques.

In the next chapter, you will learn about data logging and recording experimental work using the graphing features of the Educational Edition of the software.

9
Experiment Software and Data Logging

In this chapter, you will learn how to use the data logging features of the LEGO MINDSTORMS Educational Edition software. You will:

- Learn how to autonomously collect data
- Learn how to graph data to analyze our robot's performance
- Improve dead reckoning
- Analyze gain constants
- Learn how to write graphical programs

Graphical programs are different from the block and wire-based programming we have engaged in so far.

Data logging software

There are four major differences between the Home and Educational Editions of the LEGO MINDSTORMS EV3 software, which are as follows.

- **Cost**: You can download the Home Edition of the Software for free, whereas a single license of the Education Edition of the software is about $100 and a site license is about $400.
- **Appearance**: The Home Edition has a lobby or splash page, which is reminiscent of a Hollywood robot invasion movie, which is not found in the Educational Edition.

- **Sensor blocks**: The Home Edition does not include sensor blocks for the Gyro Sensor or the Ultrasonic motion sensor, but these can be downloaded and imported.

- **Data logging**: The most significant difference is the data logging features of the Educational Edition. The data logging is so distinct and different that I would almost qualify it as a different piece of software.

What good is the data logging software? If you are an elementary or middle school teacher, data logging can easily be a great tool. Data logging allows your EV3 to gather and display sensor data in real time on the computer screen as an oscilloscope would at an impressive rate of 1000 Hz. This could be a great boon to your classroom if you do not have any other data acquisition tools. The robot can be programmed to autonomously gather data, and can be later uploaded to the computer for analysis. The analysis features of the software will calculate the average values, derivatives, and integrals of your graph and allow simple curve fits to calculate the equation of the line. You can also write very simple computer programs that control the robot based on values on a graph, which is called graphical programming.

Many high school teachers may already have more advanced data acquisition systems, and might find the data logging of the EV3 software rather limiting. The 1000 Hz can be limiting if you are interested in high frequency sounds or electrical signals. Although the software will generate nice graphs of sensor data as a function of time, you cannot make x-y sensor graphs. For example, you could not graph the Gyro Sensor on your y axis, and your motor rotation encoder on the x axis. The graphical analysis curve fitting will allow you to perform linear, quadratic, and cubic curve fits of your sensor data. The linear and quadratic curve fits are useful, but as a teacher I would rather see exponential or trigonometric curve fits than a cubic fit.

The official EV3 help tutorials do a satisfactory job of showing you how to gather sensor data if you are performing science experiments. In the rest of this chapter, I will move beyond the elementary tutorials and focus on how you can use the data logging software to analyze and improve the performance of the robots we have built in this book.

Improving dead reckoning

In this next section, we will use autonomous data logging to collect sensor data, which we will graph and then analyze to improve our dead reckoning skills. Because the Gyro Sensor is so susceptible to drift, I know many **FIRST LEGO League** (FLL) teams who still prefer to use dead reckoning to navigate a course. Reconciling the amount of turning in dead reckoning with the values of the Motor Rotation sensors can be tedious and time consuming.

Data logging allows us to directly compare the values of the Gyro Sensor to the values of the Motor Rotation sensors over a period of time.

Let's begin by attaching a Gyro Sensor to port 2 on our robot. For the graphs in this chapter, I attached the Gyro Sensor to the caster-bot, but you can do this with any of our robots. In the following screenshot, you can see a simple program to acquire and store data from the sensors:

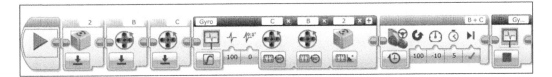

In the following steps, I will describe the program in the preceding screenshot:

1. We start out by using sensor blocks to reset the values of the Gyro and both Motor Rotation sensors.

2. We will now add a Data Logging block to our program. When you first add a Data Logging block, it is only set up to collect data for one sensor.

3. By pressing the plus sign in the upper right-hand corner of the block, you can add additional sensors. We will collect data at a rate of 100 Hertz or 100 points per second.

4. Make sure the Gyro Sensor is set for port 2, and the Motor Rotation sensors are set for ports B and C.

5. Lastly, you need to name the data file to which we will store the data. In this case, I will name the file Gyro.

6. Next, we will add in a Motor block to move the robot about half a turn.

7. At the end of our program, we want to tell our robot to stop collecting data and close the file with a Data Logging block set to Stop.

After we have downloaded and executed the preceding program, our robot should have turned and collected sensor data into a stored file called Gyro. We will now upload and analyze this data. Unfortunately, the data logging software will not allow us to graph the value of the rotation sensor as a function of the Gyro Sensor. The graphing software will graph them both as a function of time. We can then do a calculation to find the relative increase in both values.

Instead of starting a new program, we will start a new experiment. When you first start an experiment, the software defaults to the Oscilloscope mode and will graph the values of the attached sensors in real time.

We will not be using the Oscilloscope mode in this book, so you can click on the Stop Oscilloscope Mode button as we can see in the following screenshot:

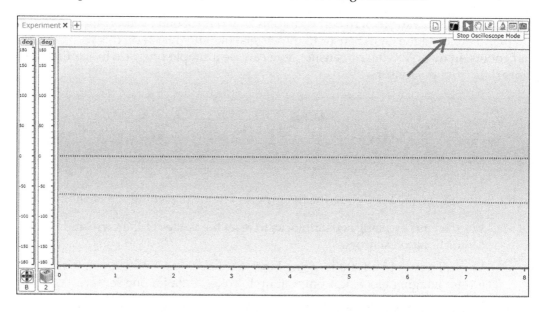

Another important difference between an EV3 program and an EV3 experiment can be found in the lower right-hand corner of the hardware page as shown in the following screenshot. The download buttons are the same in the program and experiment software. However, the EV3 experiment has an Upload button, which allows us to upload a data file from the EV3 brick and import the file into the data logging software.

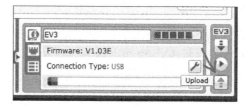

After you select the upload button, we can import a data file from the EV3 brick, the SD card, or your computer. You want to select the desired dataset and press the **Import** button. As you can see in the following screenshot, if we run our program several times, the name of the file is appended with a version number so that the data is not rewritten over each time you run the program.

If you are unsure of which version of data you want to import, there is a timestamp and a preview of the graph is shown in the window before you click on **Import**.

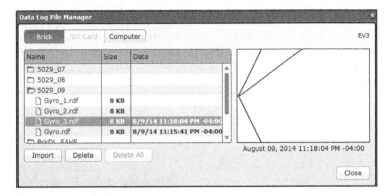

After you import the data file, you will see a graph of the data as in the following screenshot. By default, each type of sensor is graphed in its own color, which we can change later. For instance, both rotation sensors are of the same color, which makes it difficult to differentiate between them. Also, by default, the individual data points are not shown, only the lines between the points are. We will also want to scale the axes of our graph, so we do not have wasted space in the graph.

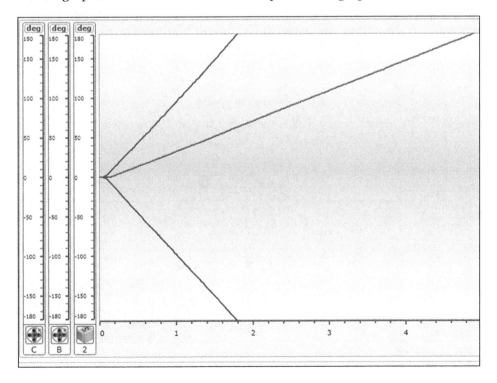

There are four data logging tabs in the lower left-hand corner of the screen. By clicking on the Dataset Table tab, you are shown each dataset. There is a scroll bar underneath the dataset values, and by scrolling to the right, you can see the values for all the collected data. If you are accustomed to using a conventional vertically-based spreadsheet, it might be a bit awkward to scroll left and right to search through a list of values. Fortunately, you can export the data in a .csv format by navigating to **Tools | Export Datasets** if you want to use your own spreadsheet software.

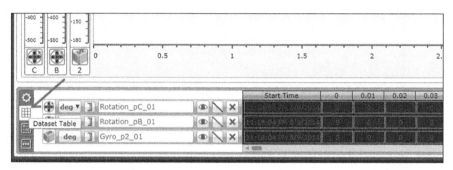

By clicking on the Color and Plot Style button (which, by default, is a forward slash), the Color and Plot Style window will pop up. This allows us to change the color of an individual dataset. We can also display the individual data points with circles, squares, and crosses. If you have a limited number of data points in the time period shown, this can work fine; otherwise, the icons will blur together making a thick line.

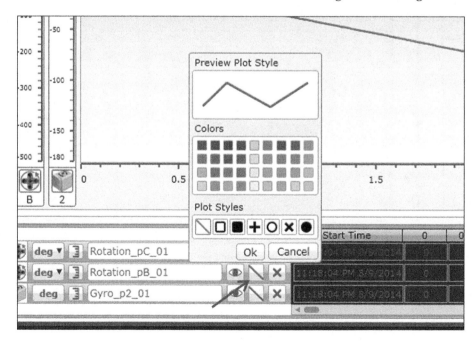

By clicking on the axes values, I can manually rescale the axes. In the following screenshot, I chose to redisplay time from 0 to 5 seconds. I kept the Gyro Sensor the same, but redisplayed the Motor Rotation sensors from -500 to 500 degrees. A lack of symmetry in the axes will cause an offset in the zero point of the graph. In this graph, we can see that the rotation sensor connected to port B is constantly increasing in a negative direction, whereas the other rotation sensor and the Gyro Sensor are constantly increasing in a positive direction.

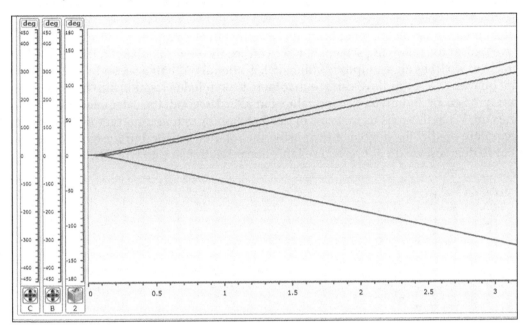

In the preceding screenshot, we can clearly see how the Gyro Sensor values and Motor Rotation sensor values are proportional to each other. If we want to numerically determine the constant of proportionality, we will need to calculate a new dataset. By clicking on the Dataset Calculation tab of the data logging tabs, you can calculate and create a new dataset based on any previously created datasets. There is a wealth of mathematical functions available from simple arithmetic functions to trigonometry, logarithms, and calculus. The ease of use is a significant strength of the software. In our case, we are interested in finding the constant of proportionality between the Gyro Sensor values and the motor rotation values. By clicking on the appropriate datasets, you can divide the Gyro Sensor dataset by the port C rotation sensor dataset to create a new calculated dataset.

You can see in the following screenshot that `Calculated_Dataset` is
`Gyro_p2_01/ Rotation_pC_01`:

After creating the calculated dataset, it is graphed in our graphing window.
If we look at the following screenshot, we can see the new calculated dataset,
which approaches an asymptotic value of 0.35 after about half a second. During the
first quarter of a second, we can see that there is no reliable relationship between
the Gyro Sensor and motor sensor value, but after 1 second, the calculated dataset is
constant. What this tells us in terms of dead reckoning is that for larger turns we can
accurately predict the degree of turn using the rotation sensor, but for turns of less
than 10 degrees, we do not have a reliable linear relationship to work with.

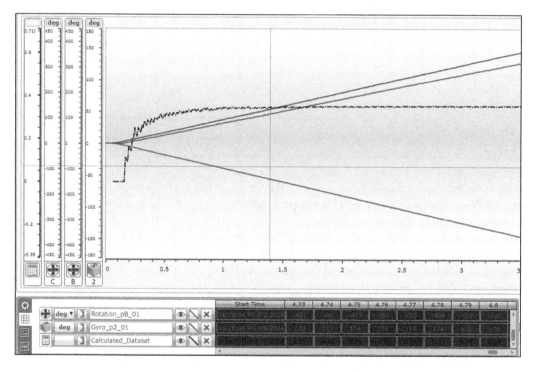

We can be more explicit if we use the analysis tool. By navigating to **Analysis |
Section Analysis** we are presented with information on the region of interest.
Specifically, the mean value of our calculated dataset is 0.35. In order to determine
our angle of rotation using dead reckoning, we can multiply the Motor Rotation
sensor by 0.35. This works effectively for any angle greater than 10 degrees.

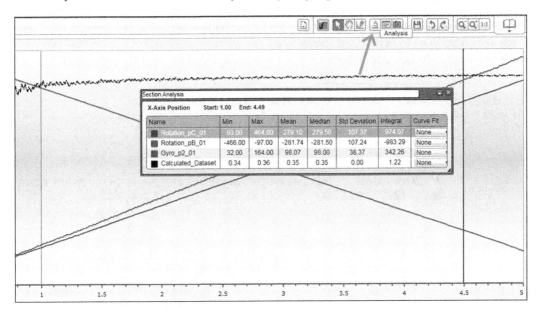

Although, by traditional discrete methods you probably could have determined this
proportionality constant, the data logging software has enabled us to quantitatively
know when this constant is reliable.

Analyzing gain constants

In the previous chapter, we discussed proportional and PID control algorithms.
When it was time to determine the best gain, derivative, and integral constants, we
largely left things up to trial and error. Patient use of data logging would allow us to
quantitatively analyze the quality of various values of these constants. This would be
particularly useful in line tracking as we can graph the error function and corrections
as a function of time, and compare this to the location along the line being tracked
(and the degree of curvature at that point).

In the following program, we are going to analyze the performance of a simple proportional line tracker similar to the one we used in *Chapter 8, Advanced Programming and Control*. After resetting the motor rotation sensors, we use a Data Logging block to record values from the Color Sensor and the Motor Rotation sensors. We are recording the Reflected Light Intensity of the Color Sensor, which is plugged into port 3. Instead of recording the positions of the Motor Rotation sensors, we are measuring the current power values of the Motor sensors. The reason for this is we are curious as to how hard the motors are working to correct the errors. We want to monitor these values because they are the output of the PID controller.

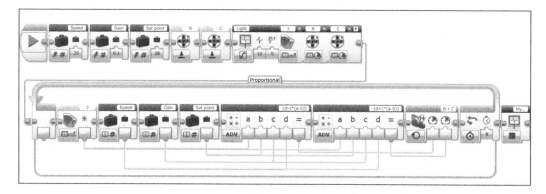

The graph in the following screenshot is an example of data from the preceding program. The Light Sensor values are marked with crosses. The motor current and power values are marked with circles and squares respectively. As you can see, the values of the motor currents are always opposite of a constant value of about -20 percent. In the following screenshot, the rate of data acquisition is at 10 Hz, but by increasing the data rate, you will have smoother curves. I won't spend much time analyzing this particular graph, but I present this as an example of how you could quantitatively observe the affects of changing gain parameters as opposed to qualitatively observing the affects of changing gain parameters on the motion of the robot.

With full PID control, this type of analysis would be even more valuable.

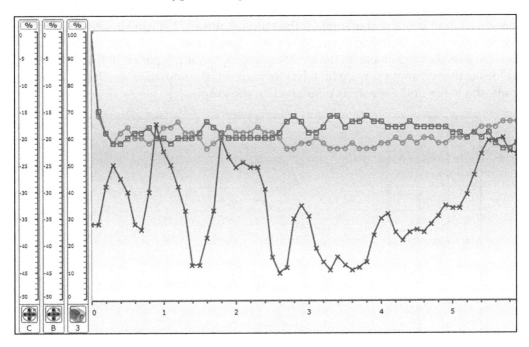

Graphical programming

The graphical programming features allow you to write simple programs based on sensor (or calculated) values on a graph. Unfortunately, you are limited to only the Action blocks, which include controlling the motors, the brick display, the brick lights, and the speaker. Again, the EV3 tutorials do a satisfactory job of explaining some elementary uses of the graphical programming. For instance, LEGO describes how to use the value of the temperature sensor to control a fan. One particular use of the graphical programming, which I like, is to program a three-level bang-bang controller. With the normal EV3 programs, this takes a few additional steps, but is rather straightforward with graphical programming. This also makes the concept of a setpoint and a bang-bang controller easy to understand for the most novice of students.

In the following screenshot, we see a graphical program using Reflected Light Intensity from our Color Sensor. The graph is broken into three regions. When the sensor reading is in the star zone, or the value is above 42, it executes the blocks in the star zone programming panel. When the sensor reading is below 38, the circle zone, it executes the blocks in the circle zone programming panel. Between the two values is the rectangle zone, which has its own set of commands. As the program runs, the value of the sensor is displayed on the graph.

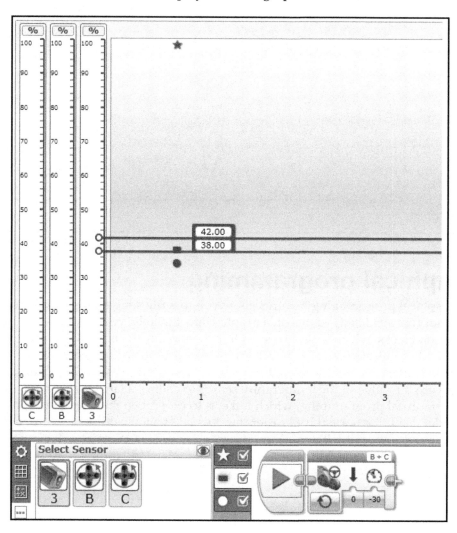

In the following screenshot, we have the programming panels for each of the three zones, the star, the rectangle, and the circle zones. In the star zone, the robot turns left onto the line. In the circle zone, the robot turns right off of the line. In the rectangle zone, the robot drives straight. You may find that it can be challenging to program the setpoints for the zones very close to each other. To view the results on a graph, you will have to rescale the y axis of your graph. In addition to the viewing, the robot will struggle to maintain a narrow range of values at high speeds and may oscillate around the rectangle zone.

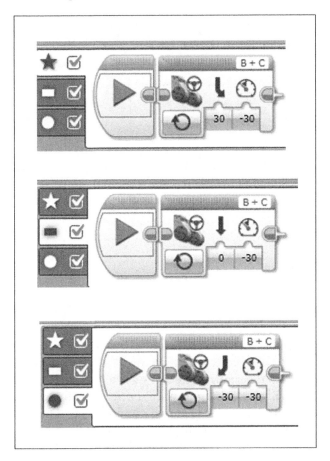

Other bang-bang controllers

In the following graphical program, instead of the Color Sensor, a Gyro Sensor is used to control the zones. One major difference you may notice is the discreteness of this graph. This is because the Gyro Sensor readings are not continuous but are only measured to the nearest degree. In this case, I spaced the circle and star zones two degrees apart. From the graph, you can see that the robot started to oscillate around the rectangular zone, but eventually settled down.

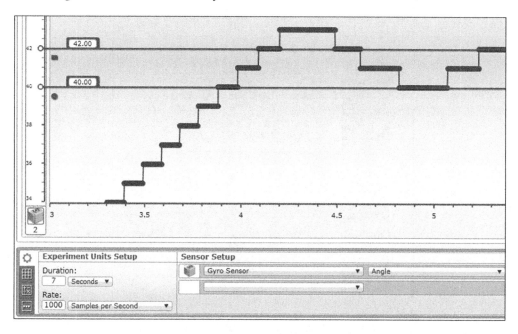

In this graphical program, as you can see from the programming panels in the following screenshot, the robot is attempting to drive at a given angle. In the star zone, the robot will turn to the right, in the circle zone it will turn to the left, and in the rectangular zone it will drive straight. Another distinct advantage of using a graphical program is the trouble with negative numbers. From the default position of zero degrees, if a robot turns to the left, the Gyro Sensor will present a negative value. Using the traditional programming methods, it can be tricky to eliminate errors due to negative numbers in your program. Traditionally, you would use a Switch block determined by the sensor value being above or below the setpoint. When your setpoint is negative, you need to account for this in your programming. With graphical programming, you do not have to worry if your setpoint is negative.

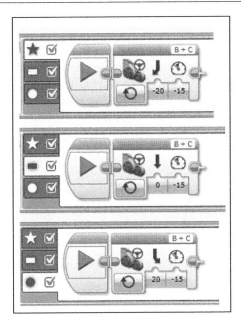

In another example of graphical programming, I used the Infrared Sensor detecting a heading to the beacon. If you want the robot to move towards the beacon, you can write a simple program where the rectangular zone is centered around a heading of zero. Again, after some initial overshoot, you can see that the robot settles into the rectangular zone.

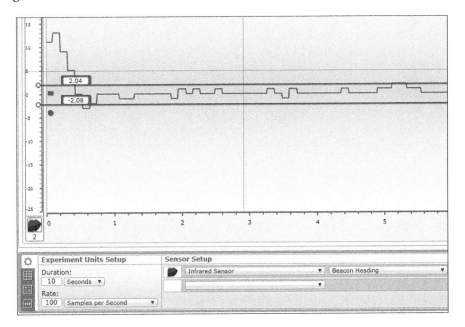

Summary

In this chapter, you learned how to use the data logging features of the EV3 software. You learned how to quantitatively improve your dead reckoning skills using data logging. You also learned how you would analyze the proportional gain constants by looking at graphs of the sensor values. Lastly, you learned how to write simple three-level controllers using graphical programming.

In the next chapter, we will explore other programming languages for the EV3 hardware.

10
Other Programming Languages

There are numerous programming languages that we can use with EV3. Two of the most popular are LabVIEW and RobotC. This is due in large part because of the student robotics competitions such as **For Inspiration and Recognition of Science and Technology (FIRST)** robotics, where both LabVIEW and RobotC are approved languages. Both of these programming languages must be purchased but do allow a higher level of programming than the EV3 LEGO MINDSTORMS language, which is written by LEGO and National Instruments. The more serious EV3 enthusiasts will do their programming in leJOS (Java), MonoBrick (.NET languages—C#, VB, F#), or ev3dev (which allows you to use Python, C, C++, and numerous others). In this chapter, we will have a brief overview of LabVIEW and RobotC. We will cover the following topics:

- The LabVIEW language, which includes:
    - Front Panel and Block Diagrams
    - Programming blocks
    - Robot tools
    - SubVIS

- The RobotC language, which includes:
    - Commands
    - Remote control
    - Graphical programming

LabVIEW

LabVIEW is a higher-level programming language used widely in science and engineering. LabVIEW is made by National Instruments, who, with LEGO, created both EV3 and its immediate predecessor, NXT. The entire EV3 LEGO MINDSTORMS software is based on LabVIEW and is meant to be a kid-friendly version of the more advanced software. There are middle schools, which have LabVIEW integrated into their curriculum so that the learning curve is not that high. You can find copies of the student edition of LabVIEW for under $50, which is a bargain compared to the full professional edition that is over $1,000! For this chapter, I used the 2014 version of LabVIEW with the LEGO MINDSTORMS add-on modules. LabVIEW works fine on both Macs and PCs. The EV3 add-ons were released in the fall of 2014. At the time of writing this book, not all of the NXT features were fully updated for EV3.

When you first start a robot project in LabVIEW you use the Schematic Editor to assign the EV3 ports to your sensors and motors. In the following screenshot, you can see how I have assigned the motors to ports B and C, a Touch Sensor to port 1, an Ultrasonic Sensor to port 2, and a Color Sensor to port 3. On the left-hand side in the following screenshot, you can see controls to use the Schematic Editor to make individual motors move a certain amount. I have found this very useful in making sure that the mechanical aspects of my robot are solid without worrying about the programming.

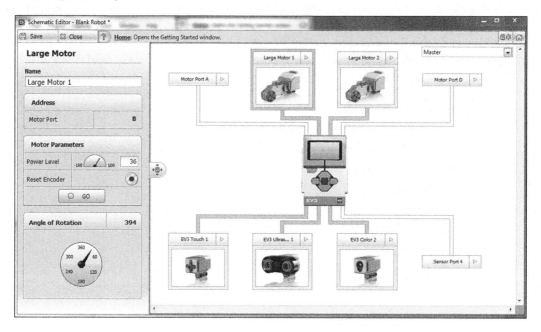

You can also get feedback from the sensors. In the preceding screenshot, you can see how the values for the motor encoders are displayed. You can actually assign names to the motors, instead of calling them by the default names such as **Large Motor 1**. In the following screenshot, the Schematic Editor is focusing on the Ultrasonic Sensor. You can see a graph of the distance measurements coming back from the Ultrasonic Sensor.

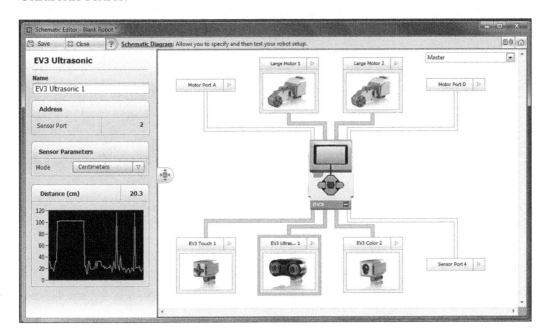

The Schematic Editor is similar to the Port View in the EV3 MINDSTORMS software. In the upper right-hand corner, you may notice a pull-down menu that says **Master**. In *Chapter 11*, *Communication Between Robots*, we will discuss how to allow EV3 bricks to communicate in what is called a master-slave function. The Schematic Editor allows you to assign all of the sensors for each brick you have, which is not possible in the EV3 MINDSTORMS software.

Front Panel and Block Diagram

Programs in LabVIEW are called **Virtual Instruments (VIs)**. When I think back to my early days in electronics, I remember buying Heathkits. You would solder dozens of resistors, capacitors, and transistors onto circuit boards. You would then control your electronics project with potentiometers connected to knobs and dials on the outside of your black box. Today, the Heathkit has been replaced with Arduino and other Do It Yourself electronics kits. Mistakes can take a long time to fix. If you use the wrong resistor, it takes a while to desolder and reconnect a new component.

LabVIEW is used as a virtual electronics black box. In the Block Diagram, you wire together all of your electronic components. On the Front Panel, you have your dials, knobs, meters, and gauges.

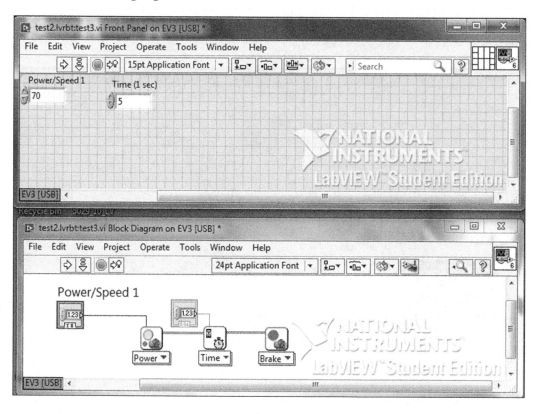

In the preceding screenshot, I have written a simple program in LabVIEW, which will move the robot forward for 5 seconds, and then stop. In the Block Diagram, which is on the bottom half of the screenshot, you can see three blocks. There is a **Power** block, a **Wait for Time** block, and a **Brake** block. These three blocks are wired together with a thick wire that dictates the flow of the program, quite similar to the EV3 LEGO MINDSTORMS software. Data wires connect two control blocks to the **Power** and **Wait** blocks. These control blocks accept values from the settings on the Front Panel, which are labeled **Power/Speed 1** and **Time**.

Programming blocks

LabVIEW is a huge programming language with hundreds of programming blocks. The LEGO MINDSTORMS add-on module tries to simplify things by only presenting the most used blocks. In the following screenshot, you can see several I/O programming block categories. These blocks control the motors, sensors, and perform data logging, display, and Bluetooth functions. You can already see the similarities to the EV3 LEGO MINDSTORMS software.

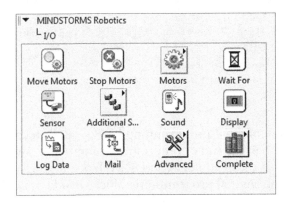

The programming blocks used to manipulate data in your EV3 programs are quite extensive, as you can see in the following screenshot. Again, the total number of loops and data types in the menu has been trimmed to the most used programming blocks. An advanced user can certainly bring in other blocks.

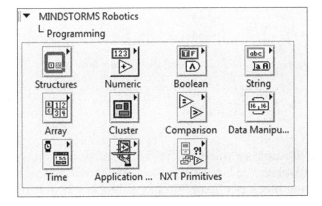

Delving deeper into the hierarchy of programming blocks, if we look at the **Structures** category in the following screenshot, we can see more than just the simple loop and switch blocks we have in the EV3 LEGO MINDSTORMS software.

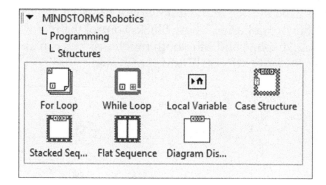

Learning to combine all of these programming blocks can be a bit daunting. To help you do this, LabVIEW has a menu of preprogramming VIs of some very common robot maneuvers, which they call Behaviors. Each block in the following screenshot is actually a full VI with several programming blocks inside of it. You can modify those blocks or use them directly in your own programs.

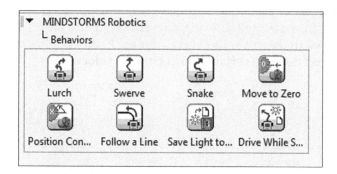

Loops

In the following screenshot is a small VI that will display motion sensor readings onto the EV3 brick display. We have a `for` loop, which will repeat for 10 iterations. The first programming block is a Read Ultrasonic block, which is measuring in centimeters and taking data from port 2. A flow wire and a data wire connect to the `drawNumber` block, which displays the distance measurement on the screen of EV3. The flow wire next leads into a **Wait for Time** block that waits for 1 second. The last block inside the loop is another `drawNumber` block. The input of this block is actually the index of the iteration of the loop. The constant **3** above the `drawNumber` block lowers this to the third line of text on the screen.

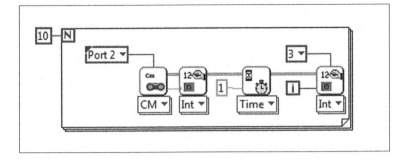

Although they look like simple programming blocks, in truth, all of the blocks in the preceding screenshot are actually VIs (or LabVIEW programs) of themselves.

Line following VI

We will now look in depth at one of the Behavior VIs we saw previously, the line following VI. You will notice that the line following VI uses several numeric functions. In the following screenshot, you may recognize that many of these numeric functions look like the traditional programming flow charts that you may have seen in an elementary computer programming class. Much of the logic behind LabVIEW is based on the flow chart concept.

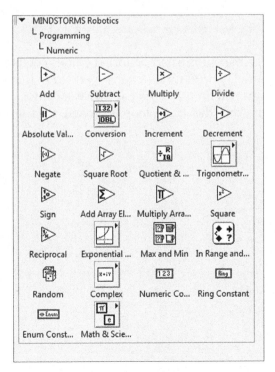

The line following VI will use the **Add**, **Subtract** and **Multiply** functions from the preceding menu. When you look at the line following VI in the following screenshot, the first thing you will notice is the `while` loop. As opposed to the `for` loop that runs for a certain number of iterations, the `while` loop continued indefinitely as long as the **Enter Button** is not pushed on the brick. Instead of assigning a setpoint value to track along, the user needs to begin by placing the robot on the edge of the tracking line. As you can see mentioned in the comment field, before the loop begins, an initial measurement is made by the Read Color Sensor block. A data wire connects the value read from this initial measurement as the setpoint and finds the difference to color sensor readings, which are made inside of the `while` loop. This difference or error is multiplied by the gain, which in the following program is approximately 0.3 to produce a correction.

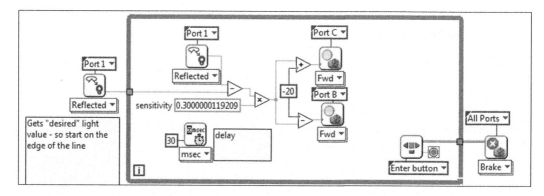

This correction is then either subtracted or added to the speed of the left and right wheels respectively. A delay of **30** milliseconds is added to the `while` loop so that doesn't run too fast. You will find that the LabVIEW code does run more efficiently than the EV3 language. After the `while` loop is broken, the robot comes to a halt.

Robot tools

Some nice features in the EV3 LEGO MINDSTORMS software are the Image Editor, the Sound Editor, and the Data Logger. Those editors in LabVIEW are even better. The Image Editor in LabVIEW allows you to upload a wider variety of image files. The Sound Editor likewise has more abilities. One built-in example is the following **Piano Player** tool, which you can see in the following screenshot:

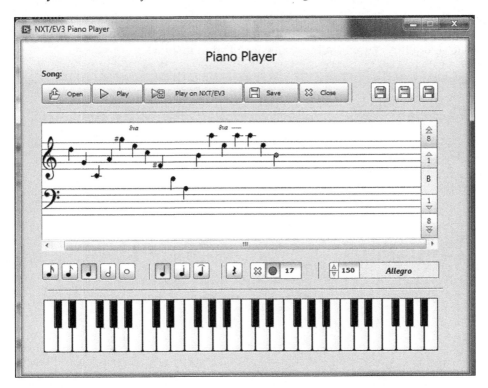

Data

As we saw in *Chapter 9, Experiment Software and Data Logging*, the Data Logger in the EV3 LEGO MINDSTORMS software had many great features. I was always frustrated that I could not graph one sensor value as a function of another sensor value on the same graph. Additionally, all you can really do with the data is make a graph. With LabVIEW, you can save the sensor data as a `.dat` file. This allows you to import the data at a later time to control your robot!

In the following screenshot, you can see a VI that takes a series of data from the Ultrasonic Sensor and writes it to a file. Another frustration is that in the EV3 LEGO MINDSTORMS software, you can only write one datum to a file. In the following screenshot, we see a `for` loop that runs for 200 iterations. The VI begins with a Start Data File block. This block creates a data file called `SonicData.dat`, and prepares it to accept distance values. The Read Ultrasonic block inside of the loop is connected by a flow wire and a data wire to the Add Data Point block. This block appends a single datum to the data file. The loop pauses 25 milliseconds between iterations. A third wire at the top sends a string with the name of the file. After the loop has terminated, the flow wires lead us to a Close Data File block.

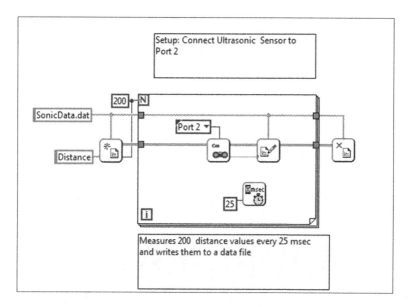

Similar to the Data Logger in the EV3 LEGO MINDSTORMS software, we have a Data Viewer in LabVIEW that allows us to make a graph of our values, as you can see in the following screenshot:

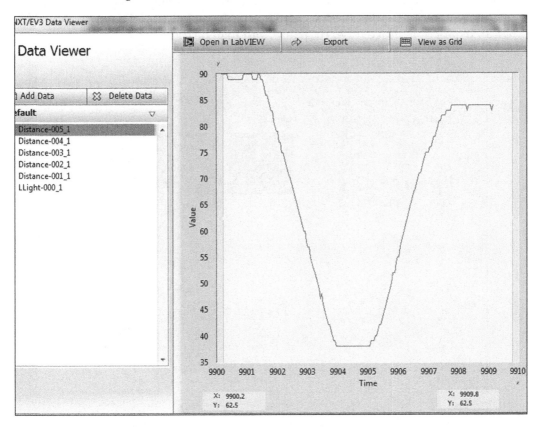

If you wanted to, you could even place a copy of this graph on display on the Front Panel of your program.

Front Panel and clean Block Diagrams

There is actually a wide variety of buttons, knobs, and sliders you can use to control the variables and constants in your VI. In the following screenshot, I have chosen a knob, two sliders, and a dial. For the current settings on the Front Panel, this VI will program the robot to move forward, pause, and then turn.

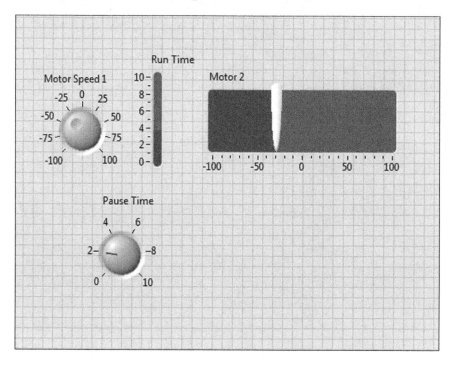

In the following screenshot, you can see the Block Diagram, which accompanies the previous Front Panel. The Block Diagram is actually a disorganized mess, which includes a broken or disconnected wire. One nice feature of LabVIEW is that with a few simple commands it will remove broken wires and clean up your Block Diagram.

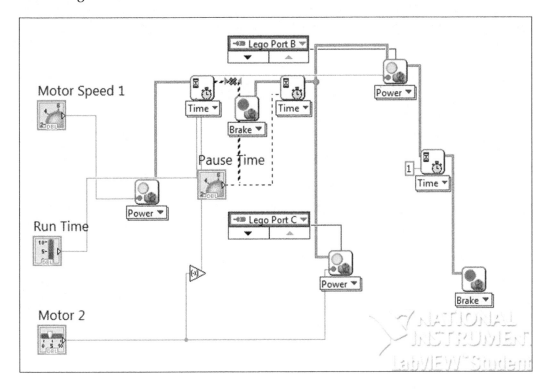

The following screenshot is much easier to understand compared to the disorganized mess that you saw earlier. The VI begins with the Move Motor block, which is controlled by the knob on the Front Panel. The **Wait for Time** block is controlled by the slider on the Front Panel. After braking, the next **Wait for Time** block is controlled by a dial. Next, you can see that the flow of the program splits as each motor is controlled separately allowing a coordinated turn. The motor slider on the Front Panel sends its positive value to one motor, and a negative value to the other motor.

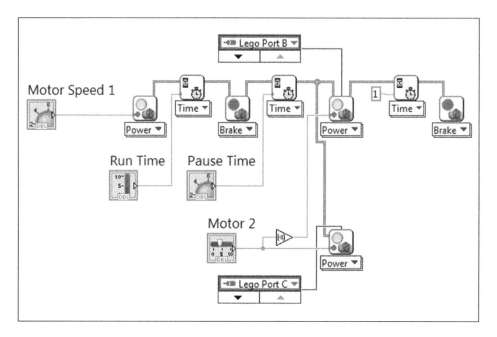

SubVIs

The concept of the My Block is based on the SubVI from LabVIEW. In the following screenshot, we can see a development of the program we used earlier in the *Line following VI* section. However, the program is quite large and difficult to view. Thus, we need to develop a hierarchy for the program by using a SubVI. We will make the entire right half of the following VI into a SubVI:

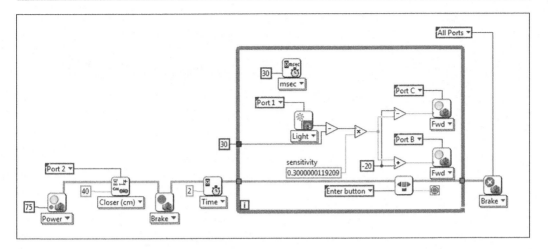

Now when we look at the program it is easy to follow. The robot moves forward at 75 percent power until it is within 40 centimeters of a barrier. It then stops for two seconds to prepare to track a line.

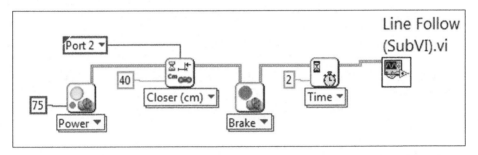

Line Follow (SubVI).vi

Just like My Block, if you click on the SubVI, it will open up and you can look deeper into the hierarchy, which is what I have done in the following screenshot:

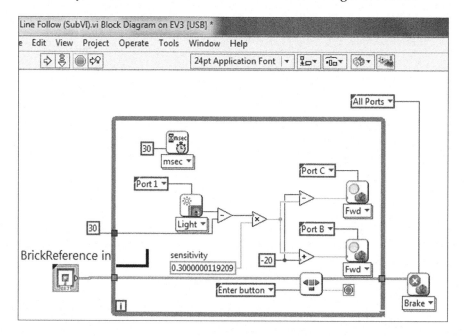

You will find that LabVIEW is used widely throughout the fields of science and engineering. Learning LabVIEW is a valuable skill in stem fields. However, at professional robotics companies, most programming is done with line code.

RobotC

RobotC is a product of Robomatter Inc., a spin off from Carnegie Mellon University and is widely used in the FIRST and VEX robotics competitions. In many ways, it is very similar to the traditional line code you may already know, with numerous added commands and functions to control robots. It is relatively inexpensive (less than $100), but the curriculum that accompanies it will double your cost. RobotC has evolved over the years and now has a Robot Virtual Worlds where you can program a virtual robot and try out your programs without waiting to complete the physical device (for more money, of course!). For younger students or those who are new to line code programming, there is also a graphical version of RobotC, which visually reminds me of Scratch. RobotC 4.0 for LEGO MINDSTORMS was released in the fall of 2014. At the time I wrote this book, I found that many of the commands, sample programs, and documents were not fully updated from the NXT MINDSTORMS to EV3.

When writing a program in RobotC, similar to LabVIEW, we begin by assigning the motor and sensor ports as we can see in the following screenshot. Although you might think of RobotC as text-based, we begin with a great **Graphical User Interface (GUI)** to set up the motors.

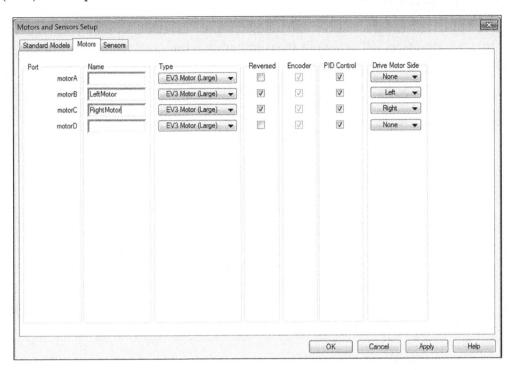

We can name the motors and assign sides, which is useful for a drive train. One of the features in this book that I particularly appreciate for the design of the robots is the ability to reverse all power signals that go to the motor. We will do the same for our sensors as you can see in the following screenshot. Being able to name the sensors is useful if you have more than one sensor of the same type and want to differentiate them in your code.

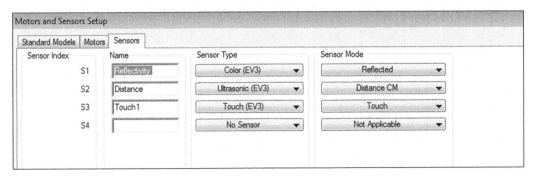

Next, we will work directly with the bricks to enable communication between the robots.

Simple code

You need to configure the sensors and motors in your RobotC program. Fortunately, the motor and sensor GUI generates the configuration line code for us as we can see in the following screenshot:

```
LEGO Start Page   5029example1.c
1    #pragma config(Sensor, S1,      Reflectivity,     sensorEV3_Color)
2    #pragma config(Sensor, S2,      Distance,         sensorEV3_Ultrasonic)
3    #pragma config(Sensor, S3,      Touch1,           sensorEV3_Touch)
4    #pragma config(Motor,  motorB,          LeftMotor,    tmotorEV3_Large, PIDControl, reversed, driveLeft,
5    #pragma config(Motor,  motorC,          RightMotor,   tmotorEV3_Large, PIDControl, reversed, driveRight
6    //*!!Code automatically generated by 'ROBOTC' configuration wizard              !!*//
7
8    task main()
9    {
10
11       setMotorSpeed(LeftMotor, 30);    //Set motor power at 30%
12       setMotorSpeed(RightMotor, 30);
13       sleep(3000);                     //Wait 3000 mS or 3 seconds before moving on
14
15       setMotorSpeed(LeftMotor, -30);    //turn the wheels in different directions so the robot turns
16       setMotorSpeed(RightMotor, 30);
17       sleep(2000);
18
19       setMotorSpeed(LeftMotor, 30);
20       setMotorSpeed(RightMotor, 30);
21       sleep(4000);
22
23    }
```

Beyond the configuration lines at the beginning of our program, if you know C, you should be able to follow this program:

```
#pragma config(Sensor, S1,      Reflectivity,    sensorEV3_Color)
#pragma config(Motor,motorB,LeftMotor,tmotorEV3_Large, PIDControl,
   reversed, driveLeft, encoder)
#pragma config(Motor,  motorC, RightMotor,tmotorEV3_Large,
   PIDControl, reversed, driveRight, encoder)
//*!!Code automatically generated by'ROBOTC'configuration wizard!!*//

task main()
{
  setMotorSpeed(LeftMotor, 30);
  //Set motor power at 30%
  setMotorSpeed(RightMotor, 30);
  sleep(3000);
```

```
    //Wait 3000 mS or 3 seconds before moving on
    setMotorSpeed(LeftMotor, -30);
    //turn the wheels in different directions so the robot turns
    setMotorSpeed(RightMotor, 30);
    sleep(2000);
    setMotorSpeed(LeftMotor, 30);
    setMotorSpeed(RightMotor, 30);
    sleep(4000);
}
```

In the preceding program, there are many new commands that are unique to RobotC such as `setMotorSpeed` and `sleep`. Fortunately, you do not need to memorize these commands. RobotC allows you to graphically drag these commands into your code as you can see in the following screenshot:

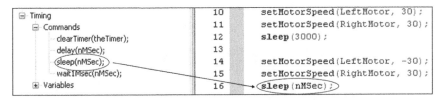

You literally click on the word **sleep(nMsec)** with your mouse and drag it into your program. You then adjust the time parameter, which is measured in milliseconds. Similarly, in the following screenshot I have dragged the **setMotor** command:

You then adjust the parameters with the name you gave each motor and the percentage of power.

Commands

Most of the common control structures you find in C are actually in the graphical toolbars to make it easier to drag commands into your program. In the following screenshot, you can see the list of **Control Structures** that can be dragged into your program:

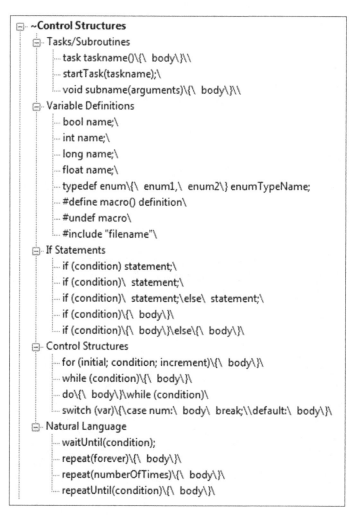

In the following screenshot are examples of many of the motor commands:

Similar to LabVIEW, many of the common behaviors have been written as commands, which can be incorporated into your larger programs. In the preceding screenshot, one behavior you can see is **Line Tracking**. The line tracking function is essentially a bang-bang or two-speed controller. The four parameters are the sensor name, the setpoint (threshold), and the speeds of the leading and trailing motors. In the following program, you can see this function being used. Again, the program begins with configuring the sensors before entering the main part of the program:

```
#pragma config(Sensor, S3,      colorSensor,      sensorEV3_Color)
#pragma config(Motor,  motorB, rightMotor, tmotorEV3_Large,
   PIDControl, reversed, driveRight, encoder)
#pragma config(Motor,  motorC, leftMotor, tmotorEV3_Large,
   PIDControl, reversed, driveLeft, encoder)

task main()
{
```

```
  repeat (forever) {
    lineTrackRight(S3, 37, 25, 0);
  }
}
```

Variables

In the EV3 LEGO MINDSTORMS software, all of the variables are global variables. In RobotC, you can differentiate between local variables and global variables. Global variables are defined at the beginning of a program and maintain their values throughout. Local variables are only used within a subroutine and cannot be passed to the main program. A discussion of pointers is beyond the scope of this text, save to say you have the full power of C at your disposal. In the following program, I have adapted a model for the proportional line follower. It is worth noting the use of global versus local variables. Another key difference is math functions. With the EV3 LEGO MINDSTORMS software, you were limited to four inputs for an advanced math function. In C, you have no limits:

```
#pragma config(Sensor, S1,      reflect,            sensorEV3_Color)
#pragma config(Motor,  motorB, rightMOT,       tmotorEV3_Large,
  PIDControl, reversed, encoder)
#pragma config(Motor,  motorC,            leftMOT,
  tmotorEV3_Large, PIDControl, reversed, encoder)
//*!!Code automatically generated by 'ROBOTC' configuration
  wizard!!*//
int speed = 30;     //global variables
float gain = 0.3;
int setpoint = 30;
int lowest = 100;
int highest = 0;
void scanLine()    //a subroutine (or MyBlock)
{
  motor[rightMOT] = 10;     //local variables
  motor[leftMOT] = -10;
  time1[T1] = 0;
  while(time1[T1] < 1500)
  {
    if (SensorValue[reflect] > highest)
    {
      highest = SensorValue[reflect];
    }
    if (SensorValue[reflect] < lowest)
    {
      lowest = SensorValue[reflect];
    }
  }
```

```
  setpoint = (highest - lowest) / 2;
  motor[rightMOT] = 0;
  motor[leftMOT] = 0;
}
task main()  //beginning of the main program
{
  float error; //local variables in main program
  scanLine();  //calling the subroutine
  sleep(2000);
  while (true)
  {
    error = SensorValue[reflect] - setpoint;
    motor[leftMOT] = speed - round(error * gain);
    motor[rightMOT] = speed + round(error * gain);
    wait1Msec(50);
  }
}
```

Remote control

Because RobotC is used in numerous robotics competitions, it actually has a GUI for setting up a Joystick Control in the software. This allows you to control your EV3 with the joystick!

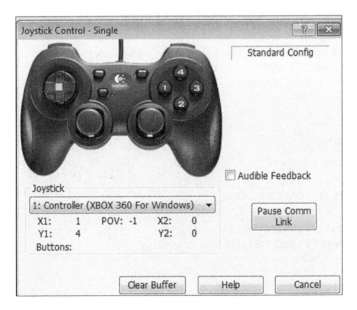

Graphical programming

As I mentioned earlier, there is a newer version of RobotC that is graphical. Instead of the wires visual programming such as LabVIEW, this is block-based visual programming similar to Scratch. You drag commands from the Command menu on the left part of the screen to the programming palette as you can see in the following screenshot:

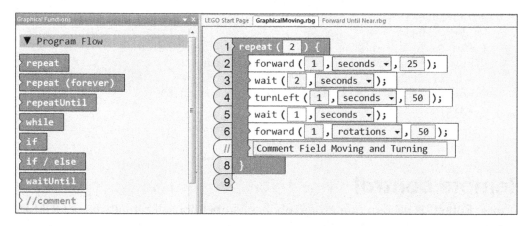

Then, with the click of a few buttons, you can convert your graphical images into actual line code as you can see in the following program. You can compare the program to the preceding graphical screenshots:

```
#pragma config(Motor,  motorB,            leftMotor,
  tmotorEV3_Large, PIDControl, reversed, driveLeft, encoder)
#pragma config(Motor,  motorC,            rightMotor,
  tmotorEV3_Large, PIDControl, reversed, driveRight, encoder)
task main()
{
  repeat (2) {
    forward(1, seconds, 25);
    wait(2, seconds);
    turnLeft(1, seconds, 50);
    wait(1, seconds);
    forward(1, rotations, 50);
    // Comment Field Moving and Turning
  }
}
```

The number of commands available in the graphical version of RobotC is significantly limited, but it allows a softer introduction. In the following screenshot, you can see the **Motor Commands** menu:

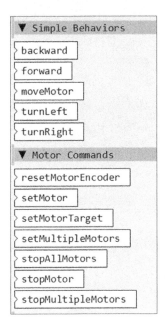

Summary

In this chapter, we were introduced to two other programming languages, LabVIEW and RobotC. This chapter was not meant as a tutorial for those languages, but to highlight some of the differences and the potential of more sophisticated languages.

In the next chapter, we will explore communication between robots.

11
Communication between Robots

In this chapter, we will explore how to use messaging via Bluetooth to enable communication between robots. We will:

- Enable Bluetooth communication between robots
- Use one robot to control another
- Program two robots to communicate to maintain a safe driving distance
- Use two robots to collaborate to find a hidden target

Enabling communication

The official EV3 tutorials walk you through setting up Bluetooth communication and setting up connections on the brick. The tutorials then move on to how to send a message from one robot to another. One master EV3 robot can control up to seven slave EV3 robots. Master-Slave robotic control is a common term in engineering. In this arrangement, the master can communicate back and forth with all of the slave robots. However, the slave robots cannot communicate with each other. There are many examples on the Web using one EV3 as a remote control for a full robot. In this chapter, I will focus on two full robots communicating with each other.

To start, we must name the robots. You can do that by connecting your EV3 brick to your computer with the USB cable. In the Brick Information panel, you can change the name of your EV3 brick by typing a new name in the Brick name box as shown in the following screenshot. Following the industry standards, I have called the primary brick `master`. You can name the brick whatever you like as long as each brick you are using has a different name. I am calling the secondary robot `slave1`.

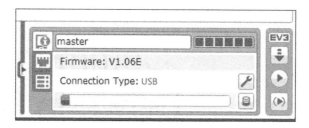

Next we will work directly with the bricks to enable communication between the robots. The EV3 tutorials have you enable full communication each time you run a program using the brick buttons. In truth, you only need to allow the robots to discover each other once using the brick buttons. In subsequent programming, you can make the connection using the software.

From the settings menu on your EV3 brick, select **Bluetooth**, as seen in the following image. Do this on both of your bricks, the master and the slave.

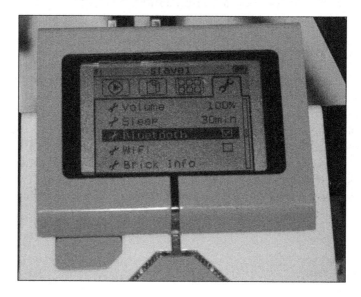

When you select **Bluetooth** by pressing the center button, you will see the Bluetooth menu as shown in the following image. You should deselect the **iPhone/iPad/iPod** option. You want to have both the **Bluetooth** and **Visibility** options selected. Do this on both bricks. Once this is done, select **Connections** on both bricks just to make sure that they can see each other.

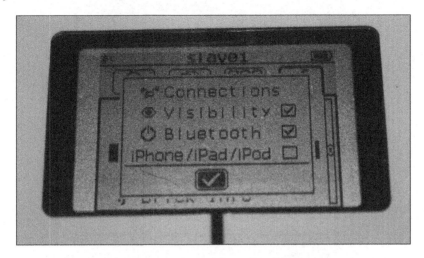

Now select **Search** as shown in the following image. This will allow the pairing between the EV3 bricks to begin.

From the master brick, you want to select the robot to which you want to pair as shown in the following image. You only need to do this on the master brick, not both the bricks.

When you select the robot to pair with, it will ask you if you want to connect. Click on **Connect** to begin the pairing as shown in the following image:

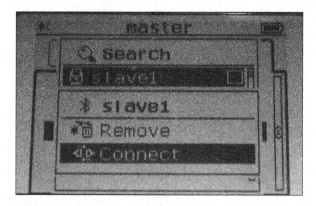

At this point, a prompt to accept the pairing will appear on the slave robot. Accept the pairing. Once accepted, it will ask you for a **PASSKEY** as shown in the following image. Make sure you enter the same passkey on both robots.

After you have entered the passkey, the robots should complete the connection. You will see the display as shown in the following image:

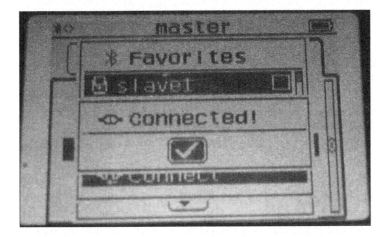

This process for connecting the robots by using the brick buttons only needs to be done once. However, if you do not do this initial pairing, when you try to execute the programs, you will receive an error.

Messaging

In the EV3 tutorials (embedded in the EV3 LEGO MINDSTORMS software), they present an example of messaging where feedback from the shaft encoders of a motor on the master robot will make the slave robot move. However, the feedback in the tutorial programs takes position readings from the motor on the master robot. This is very similar to a knob on a remote control being used to make your robot move. I will instead use power values so that we can emulate the speed of the master robot.

Follow the leader

In the following example, I used two similar robots. The robots do not need to be identical, but will need to have the right motor plugged into port B and the left motor into port C. I used two of the caster-bots from our earlier chapters. In this program, when you push the master robot along a surface, the `slave1` robot will emulate the motions.

In the following screenshot is the program to be downloaded onto the master robot. The program begins by turning on the brick's Bluetooth with the Bluetooth Communication On block. Next, the program prepares a line of communication between the master robot and the slave1 robot with the Bluetooth Communication Initiate block. Note that this allows the master robot to send messages to the slave1 robot, but does not prepare the master robot to receive messages. You need to type the correct name of the receiving robot in this block. After resetting the shaft encoder on motor C with the Motor Rotation block, we enter the infinite Loop block called `Motion`. The current power values are sent from the Motor Rotation block to the Message Send Numeric blocks. I have chosen to have one signal for each motor. Although I am just making the robot move backwards and forwards in this chapter, having separate motor messages sets up the option for you to modify the code for giving navigation instructions.

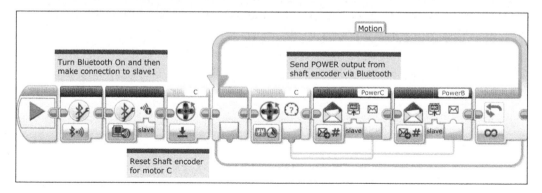

The program for the slave robot is quite simple as you can see in the following screenshot. We start out by turning on the brick's Bluetooth. Inside the Loop block, we can see the program repeatedly accepts power current value messages from the Messaging Receive Numeric block and sends them to the Move Tank On block.

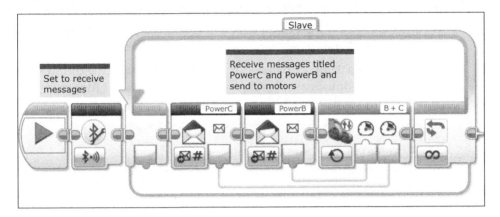

Because these are the actual current power values measured by the shaft encoder on the master robot, the slave robot does an efficient job of emulating the motion of the other robot.

Maintain a distance

A lot of the current robotics research is geared towards developing autonomous vehicles. A large part of that research is in collision avoidance and making sure the cars do not come into contact with each other. In the following program, we will try to maintain a fixed distance between the two robots using a proportional algorithm. If you remember, in *Chapter 8*, *Advanced Programming and Control*, when we first introduced the use of the proportional controller with the Ultrasonic Sensor, it was relative to a fixed target. This is analogous to the problem of stopping at a dark line on the ground using the Color Sensor. The problem of maintaining a fixed distance to a moving target is more akin to line tracking.

We will use the same slave program as we used in the *Follow the leader* section. All of the magic will happen in the program on the master robot. You will need to mount an Ultrasonic Sensor pointing backwards on your master robot. You can plug the motion sensor into port 4 on the master robot. This will be used to detect how far away the slave robot is. There will be two parallel sequences, one sequence for communication with the slave, and the other sequence to control the motion of the master robot.

We begin the control sequence as follows:

1. Define the Variable blocks with values for the gain and setpoint distance in our proportional controller.

2. Next the Bluetooth Connection blocks initiate a connection to the slave robot.

3. Then our Distance Sensing Loop block will send messages to the slave robot so that a constant distance between the robots can be maintained.

4. Inside the Loop block, the Advanced Math block computes the difference between the Ultrasonic Sensor block value and the value for the setpoint distance, and multiplies this difference by the gain.

5. This power level is sent to the slave robot by the Messaging blocks.

A simple challenge would be to add in another variable for the speed of the master robot into this algorithm, so the robot is not always playing catch up.

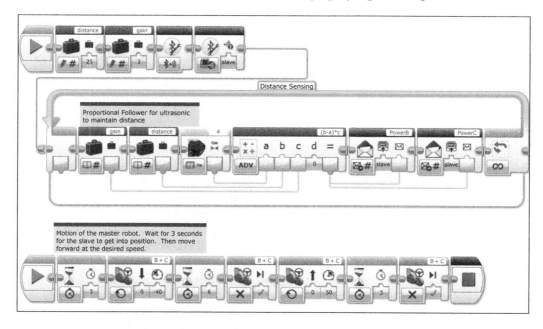

The second sequence controls the motion of the master robot. We begin with a Wait Time block in order to allow the slave robot a few seconds to catch up with the master robot. Then we have the master robot move forward for several seconds, stop, and then move backwards. Again, you should start the program on the slave robot first. When you run the programs, you can play around with the value for the gain and distance variables. You can try to create new situations to simulate traffic on a highway. As an added challenge, you could add in a proportional line tracker to both robots and have them track a line while maintaining a fixed distance.

Search and rescue

In the following program, we will use two robots to try and find a target. Without knowing where the target is, each robot will travel outwards and look for a target. When the target is found, the other robot will join the robot that found the target. If neither one finds the target, both robots return to their starting positions.

If you extend this model to multiple robots, we have a branch of robotics called swarming. How can you use multiple autonomous robots to find an unknown target in two-dimensional (or three-dimensional) space? The uses start from basic vacuum cleaner robots up to flying autonomous quad-copters finding lost hikers and forest fires.

In this particular example, you should place two identical robots back to back, as you can see in the preceding image. Mount each robot with a Color Sensor pointed downwards to look for the target. In the preceding image, most of the terrain was a white surface. But as you can see in the following image, the target is a black sheet of paper. At the front of each robot, place a Touch Sensor. When the Touch Sensor hits a barrier, it will trigger the Color Sensor to measure the color on the surface below it. Place a colored target before the barrier in only one direction.

On both robots, the Touch Sensor is plugged into port 1, and the Color Sensor is plugged into port 3. The Ultrasonic Sensor is not needed for this program, but is left over from the *Maintain a distance* section's program.

Let's start out by examining the program for the slave robot. There are two parallel sequences in this program, as you can see in the following screenshot. The first sequence receives movement instructions from the master robot. This is similar to the Slave Loop block from the earlier programs, except now I am using a Move Steering block to simplify the programming.

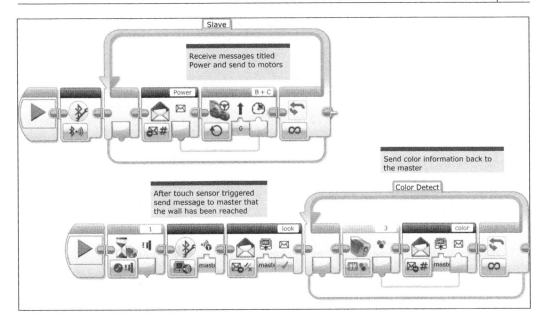

The second sequence sends information back to the master robot in the following manner:

1. This sequence begins only once the Touch Sensor on the slave robot has been triggered by the Wait Touch Sensor Change block.

2. What is different is that now the Bluetooth Communication Initiate block prepares the master robot to receive messages back from slave1.

3. Next, a Messaging Send Logic block sends back a Boolean true statement called `look` to the master. This allows the master to know that the slave robot has reached the wall and is now sending color information.

4. The Color Detect Loop block will constantly send readings from the value of the Color Sensor Measuring block back to the master via the Messaging Send Numeric block.

To simplify the program on the master robot, I have used several My Blocks on the third of three parallel sequences, as you can see in the following screenshot:

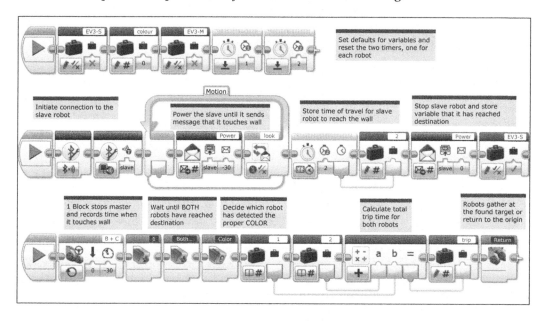

The first sequence defines default values for several variables and resets some sensor values. We begin by setting the Boolean Logic Variable blocks EV3-M and EV3-S to false (M for master and S for slave). These variables keep track of when the Touch Sensor on each robot has been triggered, and will change to true after their respective Touch Sensors have been depressed. The Numeric Variable block color keeps track of which robot has detected the target. The default value of 0 indicates that neither robot has detected the target. A value of 1 will indicate the master has detected the target, and a value of 2 will indicate that slave1 has detected the target. A new sensor we have not discussed before is the Timer Sensor block. You can actually have up to eight individual Timer Sensors all running independently. We are going to use two different Timer Sensors. We will use one Timer Sensor to measure the travel time it takes to reach the wall for each robot. We use the Reset Timer block to zero these timers at the beginning of the program.

The second sequence will send motion control commands to the slave robot in addition to keeping track of the travel time for the slave robot. We begin the thread by initiating communication with the slave robot. Notice that we have a Loop Messaging Compare block. Inside the block is the command for the slave robot to move forward. The trigger to break this loop is given when the Boolean true statement is received from the messaging send logic block called look on the slave robot. Next, the travel time of the slave robot is recorded by sending the value of the Timer Measure block 2 to the Numeric Variable block called 2. Finally, a Messaging Send Numeric block commands the slave to stop, and the Boolean Variable EV3-S is changed to true to indicate that the slave has reached the barrier.

The third sequence stops the master robot at the wall and makes a color measurement. It then decides which robot has found the target and where the robots should rendezvous. I have simplified the third sequence using several My Blocks as follows:

1. After the master robot has been set in motion, the first 1 My Block stops the master robot once it has reached the barrier and records the travel time.

2. The Both Touch My Block checks to see whether both robots have reached their respective barriers.

3. The Color My Block decides which robot has found the target, if either of them has found the target.

4. Next, a Math block calculates the sum of the individual trip times of each individual robot.

5. Finally, the Return My Block decides on the rendezvous point.

In the following screenshot, if we look inside of the 1 My Block, we can see that the master robot waits for a change of state of the Touch Sensor and then stops the robot. At this point, the Timer Measure Time 1 block sends its value to the Numeric Variable block 1 to record the duration of the travel time for the master robot. Additionally, a true statement is sent to the Boolean Logic Variable block EV3-M to record that the master robot has reached the barrier.

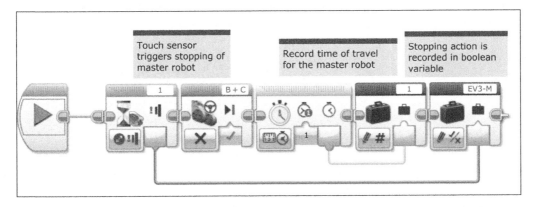

In the following screenshot, we can see inside of the **Both Touch** My Block. This is a Boolean Logic Loop that continues to loop until it receives a true statement from the Logic Operations And block. This only becomes true once both the Logic Variable block EV3-M and the Logic Variable Block EV3-S are turned to true. As the Logic Variable block EV3-S is changed in a parallel sequence, this pauses the third sequence until the slave robot has reached the barrier.

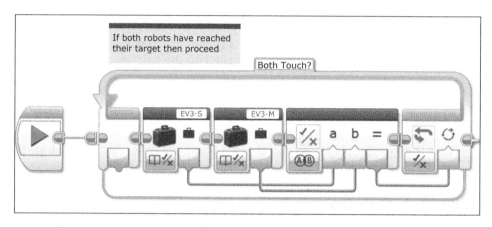

In the following screenshot, we can see inside of the **Color** My Block. This My Block will decide whether the target has been detected and adjust the Numeric Variable block colour appropriately. Remember, the default value for the Numeric Variable block colour is 0, which indicates that the target has not been found. The Switch Color Sensor block will measure the color type from the Color Sensor on the master. If the measured color is the color of the target, then the Numeric Variable block colour will be set to 1 to indicate that the master has found the target. We are not used to seeing a Messaging Receive block on the master, but this block receives the value of the slave's Color Sensor and sends it to the Switch Numeric block. Each color has a coded number, and if that number matches (in this case 1 for black), then the Numeric Variable block colour will be set to 2 to indicate that the slave has found the target.

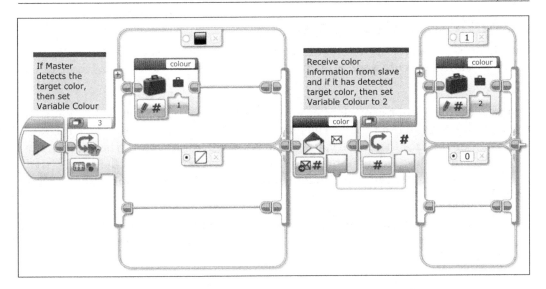

Now that we have decided whether the target has been found, we can choose a course of action for our robots. In the following three screenshots, we can see inside of the **Return** My Block. The value of the Numeric Variable block Colour will be sent to a Switch Numeric block, which we are viewing in the tabbed view. In the following screenshot, the choice for tab **1** is displayed:

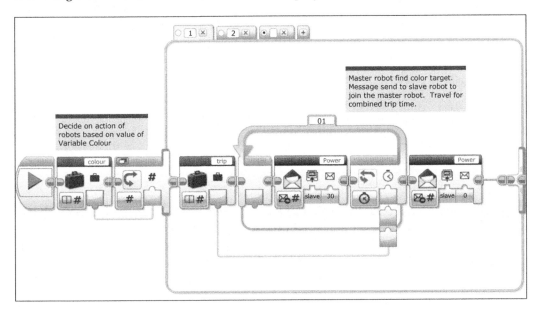

Completing the search

We will now examine each of the three choices in our switch block. Each case in the switch block will execute a series of commands based on which robot has discovered the target.

Choice 1 indicates that the master has found the robot. Thus, a command is sent to the slave to join the master robot. The motor commands are sent to the slave robot for an amount of time that is the value of the Numeric Variable trip. The value of the trip is the sum of the amount of time it takes for both robots to reach their respective targets. In this way, we can approximate the amount of time it will take for one robot to return.

In the following screenshot, we can see tab **2**, which is the case for when the slave finds the target. Similarly, the travel time is again dictated by the Numeric Variable trip.

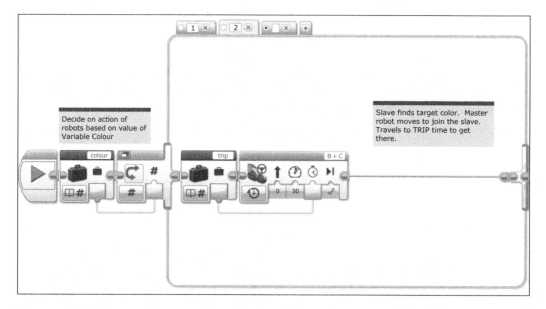

The default case is when neither robot finds the target. In this case, both robots will return back to where they started. In the following screenshot, you can see the separate motion commands for each robot, but the duration of each respective return trip mirrors how much time it took to reach their destination.

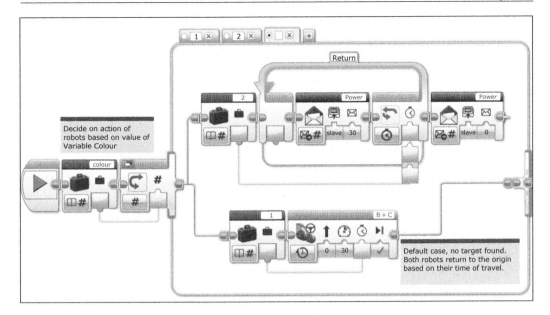

Once the robots have returned to the origin, you could send the robots out again to try and acquire the target. You could extend this idea to multiple robots, which is the concept of the swarm.

Summary

In this chapter, you learned how to use messaging and Bluetooth communication between robots. You learned how to make robots interact with each other. You also learned how to dynamically update the motions of a slave robot based on sensor feedback. Lastly, you saw how the power of multiple robots working together enables us to accomplish more than one robot can by itself.

In the next chapter, we will explore one of the advanced programs from LEGO, Gyro Boy.

12

Advanced Robot – Gyro Boy

In this chapter, we will analyze one of the impressive programs that come in the Education Edition of the EV3 software. We will look in depth at the program for the model called **Gyro Boy**. Gyro Boy is a two-wheeled upright balancing robot. Gyro Boy uses a combination of the Motor Rotation sensors working with the Gyro Sensor to balance upright. The robot also responds to commands and feedback from the Color Sensor and the Ultrasonic Sensor. This model is an amazing example of what we can build with the LEGO MINDSTORMS kit. However, the LEGO supplied program is lacking in documentation and a full explanation of the algorithms. LEGO provides the user with complex example models, such as Gyro Boy, as an inspiration of what you can build and design with LEGO MINDSTORMS. My goal in this chapter is to close the gap and explain how this model works. In this chapter, we will:

- Explain the concept behind a two-wheeled upright balancing robot
- Introduce the Gyro Boy model
- Have a discussion of programming bugbears
- Have an overview of the main Gyro Boy program
- Have an in depth explanation of the various My Blocks in the Gyro Boy program

Concept of a balancing robot

The inspiration for Gyro Boy is the Segway robot. The LEGO community has been building LEGO MINDSTORMS two-wheeled balancing robots almost since the introduction of the Segway by Dean Kamen. The real Segway is a two-wheeled motorized personal transport device that uses several Gyro Sensors to detect the pitch and pitch rate of the vehicle. The real Segway uses additional Gyro Sensors for redundancy and to detect roll (turning left and right). The physics model for a Segway is what we call the inverted pendulum problem. A simple pendulum has its pivot point at the top and the bob swings back and forth below the pivot. An inverted pendulum has this pivot point at the bottom with the bob oscillating above the pivot. We can think of a metronome or even a human being as simple inverted pendulums. In the case of the Segway, the goal is to minimize the oscillations and keep the vehicle upright and then provide movement forward, backwards, as well as turn left or/and right.

You can find many LEGO NXT Segway models on the Internet. Designing the software for a moveable inverted pendulum robot is a common project in engineering design classes. Most of the earlier NXT models use the HiTechnic Gyro Sensor. You can still use the HiTechnic sensor if you do not have a LEGO Gyro Sensor. You will find that the LEGO EV3 brick can read the values from the LEGO Gyro Sensor, which is a **Universal Asynchronous Receiver/Transmitter (UART)** sensor that takes three times more samples per second than the HiTechnic sensor, which is an analog sensor.

The Gyro Boy model

The EV3 Gyro Boy model developed by LEGO builds on the Segway designs of the numerous LEGO hobbyists. Not only does Gyro Boy balance itself using a Gyro Sensor, but it also takes commands using the Ultrasonic Sensors and the Color Sensors.

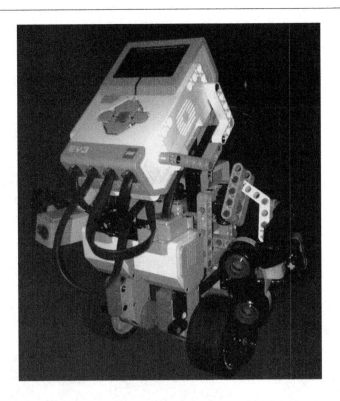

The mechanical design for Gyro Boy has many impressive features. The building designs for Gyro Boy can be found embedded in the Educational Edition of the EV3 software. If you have the Home Edition of the software, you can download the building instructions from various websites such as RobotSquare by Laurens Valk at http://robotsquare.com/. The design is well balanced and comes with a color-coded stand to get the robot started and send color commands to the robot. There is also a medium motor in the model that can be used to move the arms of the model. The medium motor uses the Technic Knob Wheel as a type of crown gear to control both arms. One arm has a Color Sensor attached to it, and the other arm has the Ultrasonic motion sensor. The official LEGO program does little more than wiggle the arms whenever the motion sensor detects an object. Although the medium motor is somewhat superfluous in the actual Gyro Boy model, it is needed to keep the robot balanced. If you were to change the physical model, then you would change the equations on which the program is based. Removing the motor would mean retuning the numerical constants in the code so that the robot stays balanced.

However, you could change the code to actually take advantage of the motion of the medium motor. One example is the modified Gyro Boy code written by Dean Hystad, which you can find on FIRST LEGO League forums at `http://forums. usfirst.org/showthread.php?20729-Gyro-Boy-Program`. He keeps the motion sensor in an upright position and only lowers the sensor when the robot goes into a tracking mode.

Sensor feedback

The three sensors in the Gyro Boy robot are used for human and autonomous feedback and control of the robot. The Color Sensor is used for human control. The Gyro Boy stand has the colored pieces built into it for just this reason, as you can see in the following image:

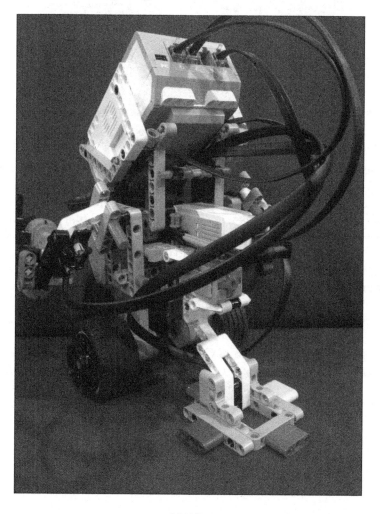

When the Color Sensor detects the colored bricks it will execute a series of commands as detailed in the following bullet list:

- When the robot detects the red bricks, it will stop
- When the robot detects the green bricks, it will move forward
- The blue and yellow bricks will tell the robot to turn right or left respectively
- If you expose the sensor to the white bricks on the stand, Gyro Boy will move in reverse

You could just as easily accomplish this type of control using the IR sensor.

If the Ultrasonic motion sensor detects an obstacle (less than 10 inches), then the robot will execute a series of obstacle-avoidance commands. Feedback is also sent to the screen display and colored lights on the EV3 brick. While the sensors are calibrating, the robot is asleep and the image of closed eyes is displayed on the screen. The Gyro Boy program does not calibrate within the code, so you need to replug (physically calibrate) the Gyro Sensor before running the program. While the robot is running, a set of open eyes are displayed on the screen. If the robot falls down, crossed eyes are displayed. After the robot falls, you can reset Gyro Boy by placing it back on its stand and depressing the Touch Sensor at the rear of the robot. If the robot never leaves the sleeping state when you first run the code, the Gyro Sensor is probably drifting and needs to be manually reset by unplugging the Gyro Sensor.

Programming bugbears

The EV3 Programs provided by LEGO with the software are highly impressive, but are nearly impossible to understand. The LEGO tutorials do accomplish their goal of introducing the reader to the blocks and vernacular of EV3 programming. The provided models demonstrate the potential of the kit for the advanced hobbyist. This is a great marketing tool for LEGO when one watches videos of the extremely cool models that can be built with EV3. However, the programs are entirely lacking in any kind of documentation. One of the main reasons I wrote a book for the intermediate level user is this need for explanation of these great programs and to help bridge the gap between the rudimentary tutorials and the advanced models.

There are great advantages to visual programming languages such as LabVIEW, Scratch, and the EV3 LEGO MINDSTORMS software. They can be just as powerful as line code, but examining the main code for the Gyro Boy program in the following screenshot, we can see that LEGO does not make use of the advantages of visual programming:

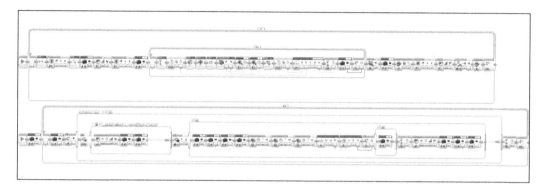

One of the leading rules in writing a good program in a visual programming language is that you should be able to view your entire program on your computer screen at one time. Although I myself am guilty of not following this, as you can see in the preceding screenshot, we have to zoom out to a ridiculous level to view the entire Gyro Boy program. Most of the blocks in the preceding screenshot are too small to recognize. Compounding the nonvisible details, the preceding screenshot shows the switch blocks in a tabbed view instead of a flat view. In complex programs, one should make prodigious use of My Blocks. This allows for a hierarchical program with several levels of depth. Such programs are much easier for the reader to decipher and to debug. When one finally zooms into the program, you will also find a complete and utter lack of comments to document the code. Sans comments, understanding the code can be an insurmountable task. If the names of the variables and loops were informative, this might make the lack of documentation forgivable. However, most of the loops and variables have short abbreviated names that are equally confusing. Lastly, the algorithms contain many numerical constants embedded inside the Math blocks. These constants actually represent what should be variables, which would have to be tuned for different surfaces or if you redesigned the mechanical features of Gyro Boy. The aforementioned Gyro Boy code written by Dean Hystad is well commented and doesn't have the previously mentioned programming bugbears. In this chapter, I will attempt to provide a road map to decipher the Gyro Boy program, which really is an impressive example of the potential of EV3.

The main program

The Gyro Boy project does contain several My Blocks in addition to the main program. I will explain these My Blocks later in the chapter. In the project, the main program is called 001. There are two separate parts of the 001 program. There is the main program, Loop M, which controls the robot, and the Control Loop, BHV, which looks for feedback from the sensors.

We will first examine the main program Loop. In the following screenshot, we can see an Infinite Loop block titled M. Inside the loop, several My Blocks are called to execute the various subroutines. Instead of one long horizontal line of blocks as shown in the previous screenshot, I have rearranged the Loop block M into several rows. In this way, we can view the entire code on one screen.

The main program loop M repeats each time the robot is set up upright to begin running. The RST My Block resets several variables that will be used in the program to zero, and also resets the Gyro Sensor, the motor shaft encoders, and the timer to zero. After the Display block shows a set of sleeping eyes, the gOS My Block is run.

The gOS My Block measures the consistent bias error in the rate of the Gyro Sensor. Gyro Sensors inherently have some drift, even after resetting the sensor. For most applications, this drift will not affect your programs, but the Gyro Boy requires extra precision. This is done during the start up sequence, so this error in the Gyro rate value can be subtracted from subsequent balancing calculations. This start up sequence may take some time and the program will not continue until all of the calibrations are complete.

The gAng variable block is set to a small value to account for the slight leaning forward of the robot during the start up sequence. Next, the robot starts to wake up as indicated to the user by the Sound block and the Display block. The program knows the robot is waking up by changing the st variable block to a value of 1. The st variable block tells us what state (sleeping, waking up, or fully active) the robot is in.

The program next enters the BAL Loop block, or balance loop. The program will continue to stay in the balance loop as long as the robot is balanced and has not fallen down. Inside the balance loop, the program first executes the GT My Block. The GT My Block gets timing information from Timer sensor block 1, which determines how long each iteration of the BAL Loop block takes. This information is used to calculate derivatives and integrals of the sensor values. The GG My Block gets Gyro Sensor feedback and calculates the Gyro position and Gyro rate. The GM My Block gets motor shaft encoder feedback and calculates the motor position and motor speed.

The EQ My Block calculates the necessary power settings using feedback from the Gyro, motor, and Timer sensor blocks so that the robot can stay upright.

The cntrl My Block takes the power settings from the EQ My Block and adjusts them with commands given to the robot from the command and control loop BHV. The control loop that runs parallel to the main program takes feedback from the Color Sensor and the Ultrasonic motion sensor. The cntrl My Block sends appropriate power levels to each of the unregulated motor blocks. We want unregulated motor blocks because we want to directly control the motor power using the program and bypass the controllers built into the regulated motor blocks.

Next, the CHK My Block checks to see if the robot is still in an upright position. If it is upright, the ok logic variable block is written as false, otherwise the ok logic variable block is declared true.

In an attempt to maintain a level of consistency in the duration of each iteration of the balance loop, the difference in output of the Timer sensor 1 blocks from the beginning and end of the loop are used to determine the length of time to wait before proceeding with the next iteration of the balance loop. A consistent duration of each iteration of the loop allows us to not weigh the averaging of values that takes place from one iteration to the next.

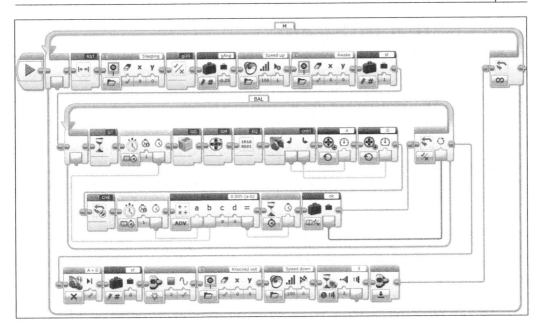

The balance loop is broken by an affirmative answer to the logic statement provided by the ok Variable block. In other words, if the robot has fallen down, it breaks the loop. The Move Tank block stops the motors and the st Variable block to set the robot to state 0, which is a resting state. When the robot is in state 0, the motor variable blocks Cdrv and Cstr are set to 0 via the command loop, which we will see in the following section. To symbolize that the robot is in distress, the brick status light block sets the EV3 brick LED to turn red and the Display block shows knocked out eyes. The Sound block generates a sound of revving down the engines. The audiovisual cues are a prompt for the human to reset the robot onto its stand. The robot then waits for the user to depress the Touch Sensor. After the Touch Sensor is pressed, the Touch Sensor Wait block allows the main loop to continue.

The control program

The second part of the program, the control loop BHV, has its own Start block, which allows this part of the program to run in parallel to the main programming loop. At the beginning, the st Variable block sets the robot state to 0 or resting. The program then enters the BHV Loop block or the robot behavior loop.

A numeric switch block examines which of the three robot states the robot is in, with 0 for resting state, 1 for waking state, and 2 for the active state. The resting state (state 0) is the default case of the switch block. In this state, the variables blocks Cdrv and Cstr are set to 0. The Cdrv variables block (**Control drive**) is used to control the speed at which the robot drives either forward or backwards. The Cstr variable block (**Control steering**) is used to control in which direction the robot steers. Setting both to 0 will result in no motion by the robot.

After the Gyro Sensor has been calibrated by the gOS My Block in the main program, the control state is set to state 1, which is the waking state. In the waking state, the robot moves slowly and confirms that it is in a balancing state, and what the upright orientation is. In the Switch block, we can see in state 1 that the variable block Cdrv is set to a slower value of 40. Gyro Boy will move faster in the active state. At the end of a 4 second delay, due to a Wait block, the st variable block is set to state 2, which allows the robot to be in the active state.

In the active state, state 2 of the numeric switch block, the robot is ready to accept commands and feedback from the Color and Ultrasonic Sensors. The Color Sensor switch block has six choices, with the default case being no color detected and no action taken. Each case of the Switch block (except the default case) begins with a Sound block so that you know a color has been detected. The following list tells you what happens when the color has been detected:

- The red case will set the variables blocks Cdrv and Cstr to 0, thus stopping the robot

- The green case will cause the robot to move straightforward by setting the variable block Cdrv to 150, and the variable block Cstr to 0

- The yellow and blue cases will set the variable block Cstr to 70 or -70 respectively, thus causing the robot to turn left or right

If the robot was previously stopped, then it will turn in place. If the robot is moving forward, it will continue to move forward and turn at the same time.

It is not obvious in the video embedded in the software, but there is actually a reverse command, which is activated by showing the white bricks to the Color Sensor. The white case will set the variable blocks Cdrv to a value of -75, which you may note is half of the forward value selected in the green case.

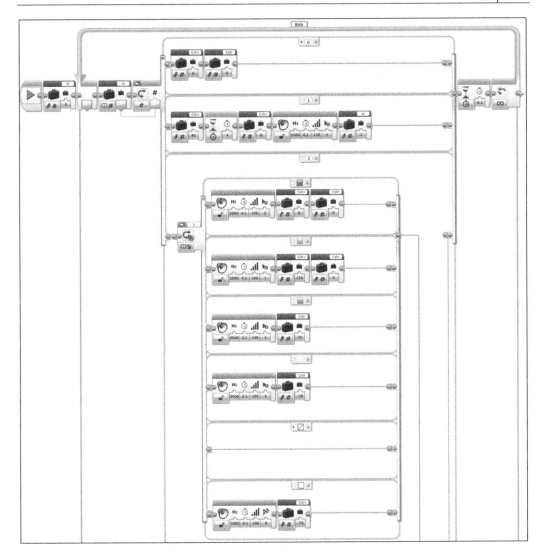

The Gyro Boy is also aware of obstacles in its path, which we can see in the preceding screenshot. After the Color Sensor switch block comes an Ultrasonic motion sensor switch block case, which is set to return a false case if no object is detected within 10 inches or 25 centimeters, and thus no action is taken. However, if an object is detected within 25 centimeters, then a case with an obstacle avoidance algorithm is executed.

First the variables block Cstr is set to 0 to stop the robot from turning. Next, the previous driving speed is stored into the variable block oldDr. The robot slowly backs up with the variable blocks Cdrv set to -10, and wiggles its arms using the Move Medium Motor blocks.

The robot will next turn either left or right to avoid the obstacle. The choice of turning left or right is actually selected at random. If the robot is caught up in a corner, this will allow the robot to eventually find its way out of the corner. A numeric random block chooses a random integer between -1 and 1. The compare block tests to see whether the result of the random generator is equal to 1 or not. Interestingly, this choice of algorithm gives a 66 percent chance of being false, since both -1 and 0 are options, and there is only a 33 percent chance of being true. This is a bug in the LEGO firmware that causes the first and last values in the range of values to have only half the probability of being selected. You could actually develop a workaround for this bug, if you increase the range from -1 to 2. Then if the random number generator selects the value of 2, rewrite this value as -1. If I wrote the program, I might have chosen instead to use a logic random block.

The compare block is connected by wire to the logic switch block. Each case of the logic switch blocks sets the variable block Cstr to either 70 or -70 to enable the turning. After 4 seconds of turning, the robot stops (by setting the variable blocks Cdrv to 0). The program next restores the robot to its previous condition of motion by writing the value of the forward or reverse motion stored in the variable block oldDr back to the variable block Cdrv, as you can see in the following screenshot:

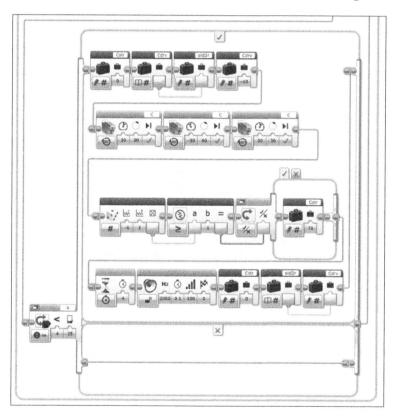

The RST My Block

The RST My block resets all of the variables to their starting values and resets the readings on all of the Gyro and Motor Rotation sensors. The main programming loop starts each and every time the robot is set upright. Since the RST My Block is inside of the main programming loop, it is not merely an initialization block that is only run at the beginning of the entire program, but every time that the robot is set upright it goes to enter the balancing loop. The My Block begins by resetting the values for the shaft encoders on both of the large motors. Next, the subroutine resets the value for the Gyro Sensor. When you look at the Timer Sensor block, you should note the ID on the Timer block, which indicates that this is the second Timer block, not the first Timer block. This timer is used to detect when the robot has fallen over. Since you cannot name timers, a comment in the code would have been really helpful here. Numerous numeric variable blocks are set to zero. There is one logic variable block, the ok variable block, which is set to false to indicate that the robot is stable. If the ok variable block were true, then the stability of the robot would need to be checked.

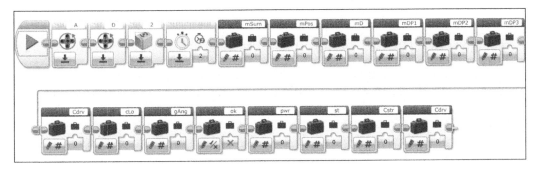

We have previously seen the variable blocks Cstr, Cdrv, and gAng. I will define the remaining variable blocks as we work through the descriptions of the rest of the My Blocks.

The gOS My Block

All gyros drift over time. The gOS My Block measures this drift and the resulting bias error in the rate of the Gyro Sensor. As a FIRST LEGO League tournament host, one of the largest complaints about the EV3 Gyro Sensor I hear about is the drift in the sensor readings. If you look at the HiTechnic sensor block, you may notice an input for a bias offset. Even after using the Gyro Sensor reset block, the Gyro Sensor may still not read 0. If you change the mode of the Gyro Sensor while it is perfectly still, it will reset to 0, but that is not done in the Gyro Boy program. The gOS My Block compensates for this bias. You can think of this as a DC offset that you may see in electrical signals.

The gOS My Block measures the Gyro offset and then subtracts this value from the calculations used later to keep Gyro Boy balanced. The robot needs to be completely stationary while the offset is determined. This could be fixed by adding a one-time delay at the start of the program. A delay of two seconds after the button is pressed would be enough to allow the robot to be at rest (no wobbling) when the Gyro offset is initially determined. However the way the program is written, you need to be gentle when pushing the brick button to start the program. Any wobbling can prevent the robot from determining the Gyro offset, and thus the robot never wakes up. In the following screenshot, you can see the entire gOS My Block. Again, the bugbear of a long horizontal program prevents us from easily understanding the entire program at a quick glance.

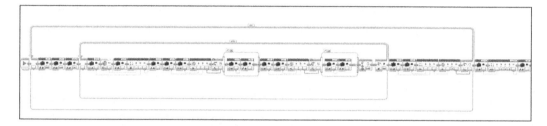

I have tried to rearrange the program in such a way that is visually easier to understand. However, I have had to split the program into two sections (left and right) as you can see in the following two screenshots. The OSL Loop block is the offset loop block. The goal of this block is twofold. The first goal is to determine the average value of the Gyro rate, and second is to measure the variation in the Gyro rate over a period of time. If there is minimal variation (thus making the Gyro rate constant), then we know the average bias level and the block can terminate. Remember that these are measurements of the rotational speed or rate of the Gyro, not the absolute Gyro angular position value.

There are several new variable blocks in the gOS My Block. The gMn variable block stores the minimum measured Gyro value. The gMx variable block stores the maximum measured Gyro value. The gSum variable block is used to add up 200 Gyro rates for the purpose of finding an average value. The gyro variable block is used to store the current Gyro rate during an individual iteration of the gChk loop block.

The OSL Loop begins by defining extreme values for gMn and gMx. These values are beyond the maximum range of the Gyro Sensor, which is about 400 degrees/second. gMx is negative and gMn is positive so that we are guaranteed to get the real minimum and maximum values later. gSUM is set to 0 because it is the first iteration. The gChk Loop block, the Gyro check loop, will average the value of the Gyro rate for about 1 second. The Gyro check loop will run for 200 iterations, with a Wait block of 0.004 seconds inserted to give some time between samples.

Once inside the gChk loop block, the value of the Gyro Sensor block is stored to the gyro variable block. The sum of the previous gSum value and the current Gyro rate are stored to the gSum variable block. Next, the program reduces the limits of the gMx and gMn variables. The variable names are confusing here because the gMn has positive numbers and the gMx has negative values. A compare block determines if the value of the Gyro Sensor is greater than gMx (which starts out at -1000). If this is true, then a logic switch block updates gMx by writing the value of the gyro variable block to the gMx variable block. Next, the inverse happens where the gMn variable block is updated in a similar manner. If the value of the gyro variable block is less than gMn, then gMn is replaced by the value of the gyro variable block.

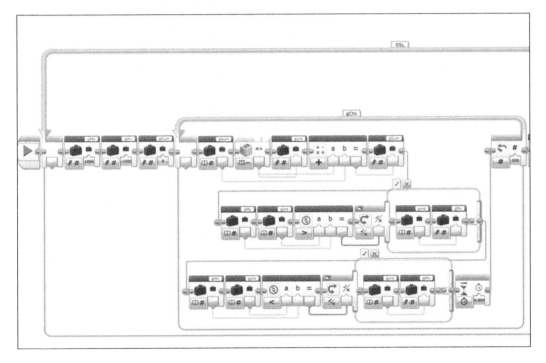

After 200 iterations, the gChk loop block terminates and next the program tests to see how far apart gMn and gMx are as we can see in the following screenshot. A Math block calculates the difference between gMn and gMx. If the difference is less than 2 degrees/second, then the OSL loop can terminate. If the difference is greater than 2, this means there is still considerable variation in the Gyro rate and the robot was not perfectly still. Thus, the entire process is run again. Upon termination of the OSL loop, a Math block divides the value of the gSUM variable block by 200. This is because we added the Gyro rate up over 200 iterations. By dividing it by 200, we are calculating the average value on the consistent Gyro offset bias. This value is stored to the gOS variable block for use in the main program and in other My Blocks.

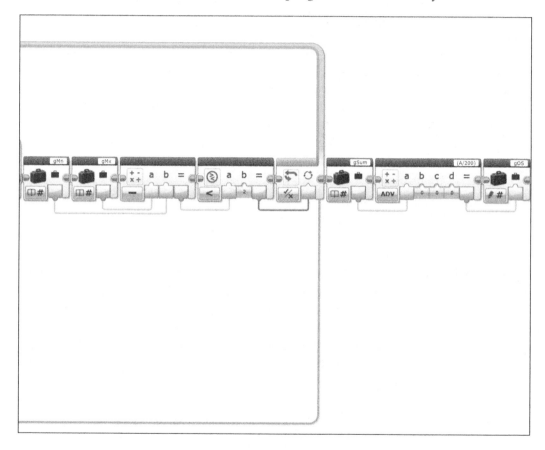

The GT My Block

The GT My Block uses a Timer block to measure the duration of a single loop iteration. The timer value is used to determine the value of the tInt variable block, which is the average period of time of one iteration of the balance loop, over which the Gyro rates are integrated to determine the Gyro position. tInt is also used to calculate the derivative of the motor position to determine the motor rate. Because the rate at which the program executes may vary, the integration time will vary. Thus, the GT My Block allows us to compensate for any affect on calculations in other parts of our program.

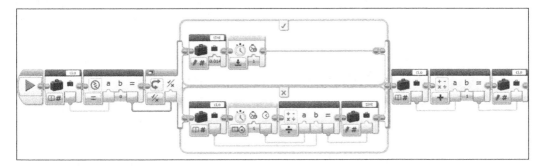

The variable block cLo is a loop counter variable. Whenever the main programming loop runs, the loop counter will be set to zero in the RST My Block. Thus, the compare block and the logic switch block will set the tInt variable block value to 0.014 seconds and reset timer 1 with the reset timer block. After the switch block, the index of the loop counter cLo will be increased by 1. In all subsequent calls of the GT My Block, the integration time will be calculated by the amount of time it takes to execute the Balance Loop block. This is calculated by dividing the value of Timer Sensor block 1 by the loop counter cLo. So, tInt is not the time of the most recent iteration, but the average of all iterations.

The GG My Block

The GG My Block gets Gyro Sensor feedback and calculates values to store to the Gyro rate and angular position variables. The variable block gSpd stores the current rate of rotation of the Gyro Sensor after accounting for the offset bias. The calculation is not quite as simple as subtracting the bias as we can see from the detailed equation inside the Block Text Field of the Advanced Math block. A new Gyro offset is actually calculated from 99.95 percent of the old gOS variable block and 0.05 percent of the current Gyro rate. This is to account for increased bias over time. It is this new Gyro offset that is subtracted from the current Gyro Sensor block value to return the value for the gSpd variable block.

As opposed to measuring the angle value of the Gyro Sensor directly, the value of the gAng variable block is calculated by integrating the value of the Gyro rate. The value of the gSpd variable block is multiplied by the unit of time over which it is integrated, is equivalent to saying the change in angle is equal to the Gyro rate multiplied by the elapsed time. The Gyro rate is the gSpd variable block and the elapsed time is the tInt variable block. The change in angle is added to the previous value of the gAng angle.

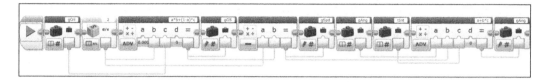

The GM My Block

The GM My Block gets motor shaft encoder sensor feedback and calculates values to store to the motor position and motor speed variables. The GM My Block does not measure the motor speed directly in the same way the GG My Block does. Instead, it calculates the derivative of the motor positions, or how much the values of the motor positions have changed over the time of the balance loop iterations. The motor position is almost a direct read from the shaft encoders with a slight tweak to account for historical variations between the two motors due to the turning of the robot. Having the current motor positions and speeds will become important when trying to calculate the needed accelerations to the motors to maintain an upright position.

The motor speed calculation begins by recalling the sum of the two motor shaft encoder values from the previous iteration using the mSUM variable block. Although the mSUM variable block is written with this sum, if you trace the data wires, you can see that the value of the mSUM variable block, which is used is the GM My Block, is the value from when the block was executed and not the current value. A subtraction Math block then calculates the difference between the old value of the mSUM variable block and the new sum of the shaft encoders. The sum is used because when the robot is turning, the same amount is added and subtracted from each motor position value, thus canceling out the change in position due to turning. The result of the second subtraction block is how much the motors on average have turned and thus this difference is added to the old value of the mPos variable block, the motor position, and a new value is written to the mPos variable block.

The difference between the two shaft encoders is calculated and stored to the variable block mDiff. However, it should be noted that this variable block is never used again in the program.

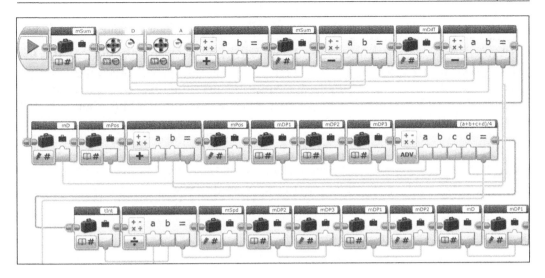

The value of the mSpd variable block, the motor speed, is calculated by taking the derivative or rate of change of the motor position. First, the change in the sum of the motor shaft positions, which we used before, is stored to the value of the mD variable block, or motor delta variable. We use the word delta for change in the value. This is added to the values of the motor delta variable from the previous three iterations of the balance loop, which are the variable blocks mDP1, mDP2, and mDP3.

The values of the shaft encoders are averaged by using the Advanced Math block to add them and divide the result by 4. This average value of the shaft encoder change over 4 iterations is then divided by the tInt variable block, the time integral for the balance loop. The motor speed is the rate of change of the motors, thus the change in position is divided by the change in time. This motor speed is stored to the mSpd variable block. In the final blocks, the motor delta variable blocks are updated to the current iteration by shifting the values of the mDP variables blocks from 0 to 1, 1 to 2, and 2 to 3.

The EQ My Block

The EQ My Block provides an equation that controls the power of the motors. This equation determines if the robot needs to accelerate to stay upright. We are solving the inverted pendulum problem with this calculation. By the end of the EQ My Block, a new value is generated for the pwr variable block (the power variable).

A series of three Advanced Math blocks are used to calculate the value of the power variable, which in turn leads to the control of the motors. Although the Cdrv variable block affects how we control whether the robot drives forward or backwards, it is the value of the pwr variable block that sets the level of motor speed to keep the robot upright. Essentially, we are trying to determine whether the robot needs to accelerate to stay upright. If the Advanced Math block could handle more inputs, then only one Advanced Math block would be needed. The value of the power variable is based on input from several numeric variable blocks, including the Cdrv, **time integral** (tInt), **Gyro angle** (gAng), **Gyro speed** (gSpd), **motor position** (mPos), and **motor speed** (mSpd). Each of these variables provides sensor feedback to the value of the motor power variable. Embedded into the Advanced Math blocks are several gain constants and coefficients, which tune and optimize the robot. If the program were well written, these gain constants would be defined as distinct variables instead of being hidden inside of the math functions.

In the first part of the EQ My Block, the motor position variable is updated by integrating the control driving rate variable over a certain period of time. A simple physics model for this integral calculation would be that distance is speed multiplied by time. The Math block multiplies the tInt variable block by the Cdrv variable block (speed). This factor is subtracted from the previous value of the mPos variable block to return a new value for the motor position.

Next, the weighted values of each of the variable blocks (gAng, gSpd, mPos, mSpd, and Cdrv) are added together to obtain a value for the pwr variable block. They are weighted by multiplying the values by their respective gain constants inside of the Advanced Math blocks. Of these, you might notice that the Gyro angle variable, gAng, has a gain value much larger than the other feedback terms. That is largely because of its primary importance. We want the robot to stay upright and have a very small (if not zero) value for the Gyro angle. The motor speed and position variables are important because if we want to accelerate the robot, it is helpful to know the current motor speed and position.

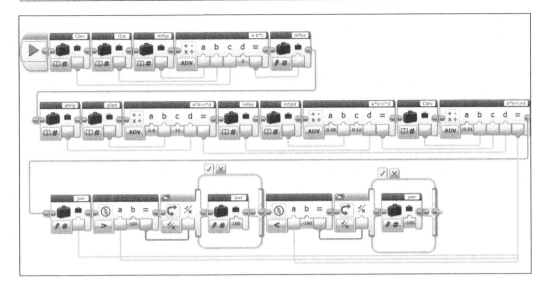

The final steps in this My Block are to put limits on the power variable. The maximum value possible for the motor power is 100. The first compare block determines whether the value of the pwr variable block is greater than 100. If it is greater, then the logic switch block overwrites the pwr variable block with a value of 100. Then, in the opposite direction, if the power variable is less than -100, the pwr variable block is overwritten with the value -100. The false case of these logic switch blocks are empty, which is why I have presented them in a tabbed view in the preceding screenshot.

The cntrl My Block

The cntrl My Block is used to control the left and right motors and to update the mPos variable block. This updating of mPos is identical to what was done in the EQ My Block, where the motor position is calculated by integrating the speed. The Math block multiplies the tInt variable block by the Cdrv variable block. This factor is subtracted from the previous value of the mPos variable block to return a new value for the motor position. This new value for mPos is used for the next run of the balance loop.

The program takes the settings from the pwr variable block as the base power level for each motor. The code then uses the Math blocks to either increase or decrease the power to each motor so that the robot can turn. Even for turning, you increase the power of one motor and decrease the power of the other. The multiply Math block multiplies the Cstr variable block, the control steering variable by 0.1, so it has a lesser influence when it is added (or subtracted) to the left or right motor speed levels.

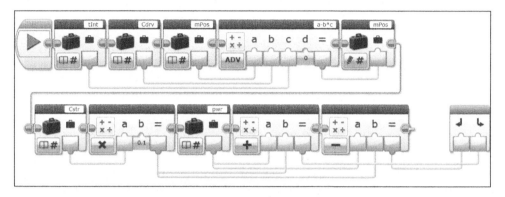

You can see the output plugs of the cntrl My Block, which are used to send the power levels to each motor. As you can see in the main program at the beginning of this chapter, there are two wires coming from the output plugs of the cntrl My Block.

The CHK My Block

The CHK My Block is used to make a check to see if the robot is upright or has fallen down. If the pwr variable block has an absolute value that is less than 100, timer 2 is reset. When the timer switch block measures a reading less than 1, then the state of the ok variable block is not touched and the balance loop keeps running. The initial state of the ok variable block was false. If the pwr variable block has an absolute value that is equal to 100 (we know it cannot be greater), timer 2 is not affected (thus having a larger value), and the ok variable writes a true statement, which causes the balance loop to end.

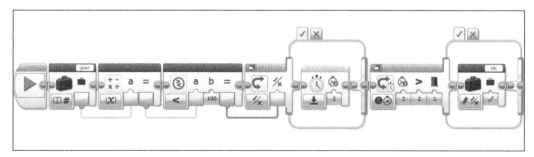

Looking in more detail, if the logic switch block receives a true value, then Timer Sensor block 2 is reset. Lastly, you saw a Timer Sensor block 2 during the RST My Block. So timer 2 was reset at the beginning of the main programming loop. The compare switch block will change the logic variable block ok to a true condition if timer 2 is greater than 1. If you remember, the logic variable block ok was set to false during the RST My Block. In the main program, the balance loop will continue to run as long as the ok variable is false. If the ok variable is true, then this indicates that the robot has fallen and the balance loop will break.

Summary

In this chapter, we examined an impressive program provided by LEGO, the Gyro Boy. You saw many examples of some programming shortcomings and why there is a need for order and hierarchy in visual programming along with sufficient documentation. The Gyro Boy program shows the potential of what can be done with the LEGO EV3 kit, particularly with advanced programming techniques.

Although you might not think that the EV3 would change much over time, I have seen the evolution of this kit since I first played with the prerelease alpha versions of the EV3 in the summer of 2012. Some of those early pieces were made on a 3D printer and the people from LEGO Education showed me the trick of calibrating the Gyro by physically unplugging it. We now know you can calibrate the Gyro by changing the Gyro modes with sensor blocks. You will not find this trick in the Gyro Boy program, which leads me to think that this was a later development. There have been subtle unannounced hardware changes. For instance, the Ultrasonic sensors are manufactured differently than they were a year ago. The new sensors have a wider cone of emission of the ultrasonic waves, which could affect how your robot detects obstacles. LEGO constantly works to improve the software and the firmware and eliminate any bugs. Sometimes these bugs evolve from outside sources. For instance, for several months the newest versions of MAC OS X failed to communicate via Bluetooth with the EV3.

Over the course of the writing of this book, I have grown increasingly impressed with the capabilities of the LEGO EV3 MINDSTORMS kit. The software is a huge advance over the former NXT MINDSTORMS software, and has many of the excellent features of LabVIEW. For the past several years, I have taught my physics classes using LEGO MINDSTORMS NXT kits with students programming in LabVIEW. The new EV3 LEGO MINDSTORMS software is sufficiently advanced that I am now migrating to using the EV3 software and hardware with my own students. I tell my students you are never too old to play with LEGO bricks. My own children, Alejandro and Leonardo, remind me of this on a daily basis.

Index

W

Wait block 139
Wi-Fi control 114, 115
wires
  used, for rotating medium motor 39-41
worm gear
  gearbox, building with 34-38

Thank you for buying
Learning LEGO MINDSTORMS EV3

About Packt Publishing

Packt, pronounced 'packed', published its first book, *Mastering phpMyAdmin for Effective MySQL Management*, in April 2004, and subsequently continued to specialize in publishing highly focused books on specific technologies and solutions.

Our books and publications share the experiences of your fellow IT professionals in adapting and customizing today's systems, applications, and frameworks. Our solution-based books give you the knowledge and power to customize the software and technologies you're using to get the job done. Packt books are more specific and less general than the IT books you have seen in the past. Our unique business model allows us to bring you more focused information, giving you more of what you need to know, and less of what you don't.

Packt is a modern yet unique publishing company that focuses on producing quality, cutting-edge books for communities of developers, administrators, and newbies alike. For more information, please visit our website at www.packtpub.com.

About Packt Open Source

In 2010, Packt launched two new brands, Packt Open Source and Packt Enterprise, in order to continue its focus on specialization. This book is part of the Packt Open Source brand, home to books published on software built around open source licenses, and offering information to anybody from advanced developers to budding web designers. The Open Source brand also runs Packt's Open Source Royalty Scheme, by which Packt gives a royalty to each open source project about whose software a book is sold.

Writing for Packt

We welcome all inquiries from people who are interested in authoring. Book proposals should be sent to author@packtpub.com. If your book idea is still at an early stage and you would like to discuss it first before writing a formal book proposal, then please contact us; one of our commissioning editors will get in touch with you.

We're not just looking for published authors; if you have strong technical skills but no writing experience, our experienced editors can help you develop a writing career, or simply get some additional reward for your expertise.

Instant LEGO MINDSTORMS EV3

ISBN: 978-1-84951-974-8   Paperback: 82 pages

Your guide to building and programming your very own advanced robot using LEGO MINDSTORMS EV3

1. Step-by-step instructions that will help you to build and program your own robot.

2. Utilize all the sensors in the EV3 kit.

3. Write programs with all of the essential programming commands.

Raspberry Pi Cookbook for Python Programmers

ISBN: 978-1-84969-662-3   Paperback: 402 pages

Over 50 easy-to-comprehend tailor-made recipes to get the most out of the Raspberry Pi and unleash its huge potential using Python

1. Install your first operating system, share files over the network, and run programs remotely.

2. Unleash the hidden potential of the Raspberry Pi's powerful Video Core IV graphics processor with your own hardware accelerated 3D graphics.

3. Discover how to create your own electronic circuits to interact with the Raspberry Pi.

Please check **www.PacktPub.com** for information on our titles

Raspberry Pi Projects for Kid

ISBN: 978-1-78398-222-6   Paperback: 96 pages

Start your own coding adventure with your kids by creating cool and exciting games and applications on the Raspberry Pi

1. Learn how to use your own Raspberry Pi device to create your own applications, including games, interactive maps, and animations.

2. Become a computer programmer by using the Scratch and Python languages to create all sorts of cool applications and games.

3. Get hands-on with electronic circuits to turn your Raspberry Pi into a nifty sensor.

Learning ROS for Robotics Programming

ISBN: 978-1-78216-144-8   Paperback: 332 pages

A practical, instructive, and comprehensive guide to introduce yourself to ROS the top-notch, leading robotics framework

1. Model your robot on a virtual world and learn how to simulate it.

2. Carry out state-of-the-art Computer Vision tasks.

3. Easy-to-follow, practical tutorials to program your own robots.

Please check **www.PacktPub.com** for information on our titles